6/82/N

WITHDRAWN

THE WORLD OF AN ESTUARY

by the same author

YOUR BOOK OF FISHES

THE WORLD OF AN
ESTUARY

HEATHER ANGEL
M.Sc., F.R.P.S.

with line drawings by
Christine Darter

6/82/N

FABER AND FABER
3 Queen Square London

First published in 1974
by Faber and Faber Limited
3 Queen Square London WC1
Printed in Great Britain by
BAS Printers Limited
Wallop, Hampshire

ISBN 0 571 10378 2

Contents

8 CONTENTS

Illustrations

※※※※※※※※※※※※※※※※※※※※※

PLATES

FIGURES

Acknowledgements

I should particularly like to thank Christine Darter for her beautifully detailed drawings. My thanks also to Dorothy Herlihy for typing and checking the manuscript and for encouraging me to join her on estuarine bird watches.

The Central Electricity Generating Board, the South of Scotland Electricity Board, the North of Scotland Electricity Board, the Nature Conservancy Council, the Port of London Authority and the White Fish Authority have all provided me with information for which I am grateful.

The following people have granted permission for the use of their copyright drawings. The Freshwater Biological Association for Figures 21 and 22 from their Scientific Publication No. 27 *Key to British Freshwater Fishes* by Peter Maitland; Professor John Green for Figures 4 and 24 from his book *The Biology of Estuarine Animals* published by Sidgwick and Jackson; The Marine Biological Association and Roger Hughes for Figure 14 which appeared in his paper on *Scrobicularia* published in 1969 in the J. mar. biol. Ass. U.K. Vol. 49; The Ray Society and Dr. V. Fretter and Professor A. Graham for Figure 17 from their book *British Prosobranch Molluscs*.

Maurice Ingram allowed me to visit his Marine Farm at Hinkley Point. My husband, Dr. Martin Angel, read the complete text and made several useful suggestions for improvements.

Foreword

Estuaries have been called the last wilderness habitats remaining in Britain, yet many have already come under heavy pressure from industrialisation and pollution. The bleak setting, the haunting bird calls and the constant changes of the scene as the tide rises and falls all contribute to make estuaries a unique habitat.

It is hoped that this book will encourage readers to see for themselves the fascination of estuaries. The captions to the plates make it self-evident that the Severn Estuary holds a special attraction for me—whether it be the white-fronted geese gathered at Slimbridge in Winter, the elvers migrating up in Spring, the plants flowering on the saltings in Summer, the Autumn arrival of waders or the majestic roar of the bore on a spring tide throughout the year.

1. *What is an Estuary?*

An estuary is a place where a river flows out into the sea. It is the tidal mouth where the fresh water of the river mixes with the salt water of the sea. In simple terms, an estuary is triangular in shape with the fresh river water flowing in at the narrow apex and the sea water at the broad base. Although an estuary can be considered as the final stretch of a river before it merges with the sea proper, in this book it is treated as a distinct habitat.

Because an estuary is a place where river, land and sea all meet, the scene constantly changes. The most notable change is in the water level, which in Britain rises and falls twice a day with the tides. During the high tides the sea water pushes far up into the estuary and recedes again as the tide ebbs. The sea water within the estuary becomes mixed with the fresh water, diluting it so that its salinity (or saltiness) becomes reduced. This diluted sea water is known as *brackish* water. As you will see in the next chapter, the salinity of the water in the estuary not only varies daily with the tide but also varies seasonally with the amount of fresh water flowing down the river.

Even the land changes. The rush of winter flood water carries silt down into the estuary which becomes deposited to form sand and mud banks. These banks may be colonised by plants and become permanent, or be eroded away and re-formed elsewhere. On a geological time scale the rise in sea level or the sinking of the land may drown a river valley, as in some of the West Country estuaries like the Tamar.

We shall see that these changes, especially the changes in water level due to the tides, vitally affect the animals and plants inhabiting an estuary. They also affect man's use of an estuary. The depth of water determines when ships can get in to a port to unload. South-ampton has a prolonged or double high tide, which gives ships greater freedom of movement in and out of Southampton Water than at other ports. At Liverpool, a half-mile-long floating landing-stage has been built to facilitate the loading and unloading of ships whatever the state of the tide.

The importance of estuaries to man is emphasised by the fact that many of our major cities are sited on estuaries—cities such as London, Southampton, Bristol, Liverpool, Glasgow and Edinburgh. In ancient times, the place nearest the sea where a river crossing was possible for man on foot or horseback, was fortified. Tracks radiated out into the surrounding country and the fortified settlement became a township. As sea-borne trade developed, so the towns with their sheltered anchorages grew in importance into the big cities we know today. In Scotland, the word *Firth* is used to describe an arm of the sea or an estuary; for example, the Solway Firth.

No one in Britain lives more than 50–60 miles from estuarine waters, and yet few people have seen for themselves an entire estuary. In addition to being bleak and inhospitable places, estuaries are also low-lying and so cannot be properly seen or photographed from ground level. Plates 1 and 47 are both aerial photographs, which were taken specially for this book from a light aircraft. Sometimes good views can be obtained from high bridges spanning the estuary. Plate 2 shows the view from the Clifton Suspension Bridge in Bristol at low water.

Bleak estuarine flats may appear to be a very uninteresting habitat; but this is not the case. The bare mud banks of the Severn Estuary which are so treacherous for walking are the homes of innumerable worms and bivalve molluscs. These worms and molluscs are the food of wading birds, which gather in huge flocks to feed, especially in the winter. On the south-east bank of the Severn at Slimbridge is the bird sanctuary managed by the Wildfowl Trust, which is the winter feeding ground of many thousands of white-fronted geese (*Anser albifrons*). These geese feed on marshy grassland areas; whereas the

1. Aerial view of Ouse Estuary, Newhaven, Sussex

thousands of brent geese (*Branta bernicla*) which come to overwinter at Foulness in Essex, feed on eel-grass (*Zostera* sp.).

In the water itself there are marine animals—both fish and invertebrates—which penetrate up the estuary a short way. A few freshwater animals move down and survive in dilute brackish water. In the region between the salt and fresh water live the relatively few brackish water species. While the number of brackish water species is low, the actual numbers of individual animals can be extremely high. There are a few migrant fish which move via the estuary upstream into the river or downstream and out to sea; several are described in Chapter 5.

Plants, like the animals, occur in zones, with bands of seaweeds in the water and bands of flowering plants on the mud banks and salt marshes. Many of these plants are the food of the herbivorous animals.

Most of this book describes the different kinds of plants and animals which live in estuaries. While there is not enough space to mention, let alone describe, every estuary in Britain, the locations and names

2. The Avon Gorge seen from Clifton Suspension Bridge, Bristol, at low tide

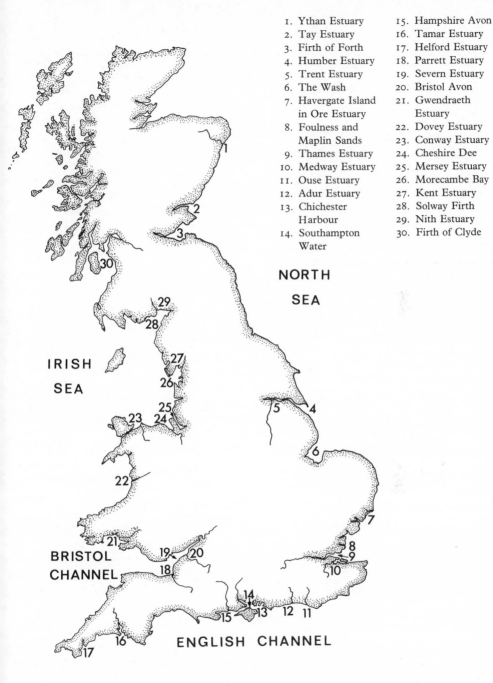

1. Ythan Estuary
2. Tay Estuary
3. Firth of Forth
4. Humber Estuary
5. Trent Estuary
6. The Wash
7. Havergate Island in Ore Estuary
8. Foulness and Maplin Sands
9. Thames Estuary
10. Medway Estuary
11. Ouse Estuary
12. Adur Estuary
13. Chichester Harbour
14. Southampton Water
15. Hampshire Avon
16. Tamar Estuary
17. Helford Estuary
18. Parrett Estuary
19. Severn Estuary
20. Bristol Avon
21. Gwendraeth Estuary
22. Dovey Estuary
23. Conway Estuary
24. Cheshire Dee
25. Mersey Estuary
26. Morecambe Bay
27. Kent Estuary
28. Solway Firth
29. Nith Estuary
30. Firth of Clyde

Fig. 1. Locations of the most important estuaries mentioned in this book

of nearly all the estuaries referred to in this book are shown in Figure 1, so you can check which ones are near to where you live. But first, in the next chapter, we will examine what problems the inhabitants have to overcome in order to live in their estuarine environment.

2. *Problems of Living in an Estuary*

Like beaches on the open coast, twice a day the banks of an estuary become exposed at low water, to be covered again at high water. These changes in the level of the sea water are due to the tides. In England we have two high and two low waters during a period of approximately 24 hours. Later, we will see why this is not exactly a 24-hour interval.

(a) *Tides*
First we must consider what causes the tides. The rise (flow) and fall (ebb) of the sea is caused by the gravitational pulls of the sun and the moon on the earth's surface. These pulls vary as the positions of the sun and moon change relative to the earth. Although the sun is more than 20 million times larger than the moon, it exerts much less pull on the sea, because it lies so far (93 million miles) away from the earth.

How is the tidal rhythm influenced by the moon? At any one time, half the earth faces the moon and half faces away from it. The moon exerts a pull which draws towards it the water on the side of the earth nearest to the moon—thereby producing a high tide. At the same time, the water on the side of the earth furthest from the moon also experiences a high tide, since the moon's gravitational pull is least there and so the water tends to flow away from the moon.

This piling up of water on two sides of the earth results in the corresponding *decrease* in tidal level elsewhere; so that midway between the high tide 'bulges' or waves, low tides occur.

The way in which the sea level rises and falls, once it is set in motion, can be demonstrated in a bath. If it is partly filled with water and left, the water settles to a smooth surface. But if the water is pushed towards one end, it slops to and fro in the bath, so that a tide-like rise and fall develops at both ends. In this simple experiment, the rise in water corresponds to a high tide (the flowing tide) and the fall with a low tide (the ebbing tide). If the depth of water in the bath is increased, the interval between the 'tides' decreases. The rhythm will be maintained only if you continue to push the bath water; as soon as you stop pushing, the rise and fall will gradually subside. Similarly with the tides, the movement of the moon round the earth and the earth's own rotation and movement round the sun cause the rhythmic pulls which keep the sea constantly in motion.

The earth rotates on its own axis once in 24 hours, but the moon is also moving, so it takes 24 hours 50 minutes for the two bodies to take up the same position relative to each other. This time interval determines the occurrence of high and low tides approximately every 12 hours 25 minutes, and therefore high (or low) water occurs 50 minutes later on each successive day.

But we must not forget the sun completely. The earth revolves relative to the sun once every 24 hours. Because high tides occur on opposite sides of the earth at the same time, the sun exerts a 12-hourly rhythm. Every $29\frac{1}{2}$ days, at the time of new moon, the sun and the moon come to lie roughly in line with each other on the same side of the earth. Almost 15 days later—at the time of full moon—the sun and the moon again come into line—but on opposite sides of the earth. At both these times, because opposite sides of the earth experience a high tide at the same time, the sun's gravitational pull re-inforces the moon's pull, resulting in much bigger ranging tides— the *spring* tides. Here, the name spring is derived from the Old English *springan*, meaning to rise. These tides occur roughly once a fortnight throughout the year, and are nothing to do with the season of Spring.

Alternating with the spring tides, are the *neap* tides (from the Old English *népflód*—neap-tide) which have a small tidal range. These occur during the first and last quarters of the moon when the sun and the moon are at right angles to the earth, and so their gravitational

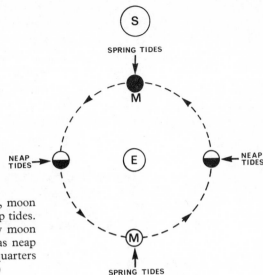

Fig. 2. Relative positions of earth (E), moon (M) and sun (S) during spring and neap tides. Spring tides occur at the time of new moon (black) and full moon (white); whereas neap tides occur during the first and last quarters of the moon (half black and half white)

pulls work against each other. The relative positions of the earth, moon and sun during each phase of the moon is shown in Figure 2.

At the time of the Spring (March) and Autumn (September) equinoxes, the sun is directly above the equator and the day is divided equally into 12 hours of daylight and 12 hours of night, in both hemispheres. The spring tides then have especially big ranges—falling to a lower level and rising to a higher level than during other spring tides—and are known as *equinoctial* springs.

This description of how tides are caused is very much simplified. To describe and understand them fully would require a whole book on its own and a great deal of mathematics. However, there are a few additional points worth noting. Firstly, sea water does not, of course, cover the earth evenly. Its depth ranges from shallow coastal seas to 11,515 m (37,780 feet) in the deepest part of the ocean near the Philippines. Secondly, the shapes of the oceans and the seas are very variable. Both these features influence the tidal rhythm. For instance, the Mediterranean—an almost landlocked sea—has a very small tidal range compared with Britain.

But even around Britain, the actual difference in levels between high and low water (i.e. the tidal range) varies from place to place along the coast. The height of the tides is measured in relation to Chart Datum (CD)—the datum used for measuring the soundings on Admiralty Charts. CD used to be taken as the Mean Low Water of Spring Tides (MLWST), but it is now based on the level of the Lowest Astronomical Tide (LAT). This LAT is calculated as being the lowest tidal level likely to occur under average weather conditions whatever the position of the earth, moon and sun. Tidal predictions used to be given only in feet, but since January 1972 they have also been given in metres in the Admiralty Tide Tables.

Chart Datum should not be confused with Ordnance Datum (Newlyn) which is the datum to which all land surveys and bench marks on the mainland of England, Scotland and Wales are related. Ordnance Datum, which is almost equivalent to the mean sea level at Newlyn in Cornwall, is determined from hourly readings taken over the six-yearly period 1915–21. An earlier datum, based on a single month's observations in 1844 at Liverpool, is now obsolete.

In Britain, the mean range of spring tides is 4·6 m (15 feet) compared with a mean range of 3·5 m (11·5 feet) for neap tides. Avonmouth, in the Bristol Channel, has the highest and the lowest tides and therefore the biggest range in Britain, and indeed one of the biggest ranges in the world. The highest tide so far recorded there was 47·9 feet (14·6 m) on 9th January, 1936, and the lowest tide was − 1·9 feet (− 0·6 m) on 6th February, 1935. This minus figure means it fell 1·9 feet (0·6 m) *below* the old Chart Datum. Now that CD is based on the LAT, low water will fall below CD only during freak storms. Plates 3 and 4 compare the view from beside the Severn Bridge at high and low water of less spectacular spring tides.

The relative positions of the earth, moon and sun can be predicted, and so the tidal levels can be calculated in advance. Each year, since 1883, the Hydrographer of the British Navy has published the Admiralty Tide Tables (see Chapter 8 'Further Reading and Information') which gives the times and heights of high and low waters each day at the major ports. It is from these Tide Tables that local times and heights, given in newspapers, are calculated. Pocket tide tables for a particular region can be bought locally from newsagents or from

3. The Severn Estuary and Bridge at high water from the east
bank at 9.30 a.m.

4. The Severn Estuary and Bridge at low water at 4.00 p.m.
taken on the same day as Plate 3

fishing tackle shops. Because the tidal wave is constantly moving, each place in Britain has a high (or a low) tide at a different time.

The inter-tidal (or littoral) zone can be divided into several distinct regions, each of which has a recognised abbreviation. The zone itself extends from extreme low water of spring tides (ELWST) at the bottom of the shore, to extreme high water level of spring tides (EHWST) at the top of the shore. Just above ELWST is mean low water of springs (MLWST); above this lies mean low water of neap tides (MLWNT). Because the neap tides have a small range, the mean high water of neaps (MHWNT) lies below mean high water of springs (MHWST).

Let us now consider tides in estuaries. The incoming tide is like a wave, in that once its power becomes reduced, by friction against the banks and the downward flow of fresh water, it gradually fades. So that usually as one passes further up an estuary, the tidal range decreases. However, if the inflowing water is funnelled in by the converging banks of an estuary, it piles up and can actually rise more than in the mouth of the estuary. This happens in the Bristol Channel and the Severn Estuary. At Milford Haven the mean range of spring tides is 6·3 m (20·7 feet), at Cardiff it increases to 11·1 m (36·4 feet) and at Avonmouth to 12·3 m (40·3 feet).

Some species of estuarine animals and plants can tolerate exposure to the air for several hours, or even days, while others will not survive being out of water for more than a very short time. Those species which cannot survive drying live low down on the shore, while those which can tolerate drying live in the upper reaches.

(b) *Bores*

When the incoming flood tide moves into a funnel-shaped estuary, it is held back for a while, before it rushes forward up the river channel as a wall of water—known as a *bore* (from the Old Norse *bara*, meaning a wave). This passes up the estuary as a wave of water. Bores occur on the rivers Severn, Parrett (Somerset), Dee (Cheshire), Kent (Westmorland), Trent (Yorkshire) and Nith (Dumfriesshire). On the Trent the bore is known as the 'eagre'. The reason why only a few rivers

have bores is that only certain estuaries possess all the features neces-
sary for a bore to form.

The height of the bore depends on the height of the tide and also
on the wind direction. In October 1966 under optimum conditions
for bore formation, the Severn bore rose to 2·8 m (9·25 feet) as it
travelled at 13 mph from Awre to Gloucester.

Bores occur in the Severn twice a day on about 130 days in the year.
However, only about 50 out of the 260-odd bores are likely to be
spectacular, and half of these will occur late in the day. The best
bores usually occur during the equinoctial spring tides and during
the spring tides in the months on either side of the equinoxes. On the
Severn, the most spectacular bores always occur between 7 a.m.–noon
and 7 p.m.–midnight.

Fred Rowbotham, in his book *The Severn Bore* (see 'Further
Reading and Information' page 121), lists the best places for viewing
the bore and also the time it will arrive in relation to high water at
Sharpness (which can be found in Tide Tables). Plate 5 shows the
bore as seen from Newnham Churchyard. Although the bore soon

5. The Severn bore sweeping past Newnham

passes the spot where one is standing, it takes about an hour to pass upstream to Minsterworth—which allows plenty of time to drive from Newnham. After Minsterworth it can be seen again, on the same tide, by driving to Maisemore Bridge, north-west of Gloucester.

(c) *Currents*

We have already seen that the power of the incoming tide becomes reduced by the banks of an estuary and, compared with the open coast, there is no persistent wave action in estuaries. But estuarine water is never calm. For one thing the level is constantly changing with both the tidal inflow of sea water and the outflow of fresh water, which increases after rain.

Water movements in estuaries—the currents—are complex. They depend on the height of the tide, the amount of fresh water flow, the variation in the amount of salt dissolved in the water, and the wind force. The fastest currents are usually in midstream, where the water is subject to least friction with the banks. However, after heavy rain, the sheer volume of flood water rushing past can scour away the banks, carrying away the mud particles in suspension and later depositing them at the mouth of the estuary.

Most movement takes place in the upper layers of water. The currents are slower, and may even flow in the reverse direction, near the bottom (the bed) of an estuary. The speed of a current used to be measured in feet per second (f.p.s.) but as the heights of tides are now measured in metres, so distances are recorded in metres rather than feet. Therefore the speed of a current is now expressed as metres per second (ms^{-1}).

Oceanographers now measure ocean currents by using neutrally buoyant floats, which can be made to hang in mid water—at any depth the scientist requires—without rising or falling. Each float contains a 'pinger' which sends out sound pulses (pings). These pings are listened to on hydrophones (underwater microphones) hung over the ship's side, and are used to track floats as they drift in the current. In this way, both the speed of the current and its direction can be measured.

At the surface you can very simply measure the speed of the current by timing how long a floating object takes to be carried along a measured distance.

Animals which migrate up and down estuaries (see Chapter 5) must be capable of swimming against any currents flowing opposite to their direction of movement. Smaller animals which live permanently in the estuary have to overcome the problem of how not to be swept away by currents. In the next chapter we will see in detail how some of these animals are adapted for survival. Basically, they either burrow down into the mud, like the lugworm (*Arenicola marina*) illustrated in Plate 6, or else they anchor themselves to rocks or pier supports like the edible mussel (*Mytilus edulis*) illustrated in Plate 7.

(d) *Salinity*

Although sea water tastes salty, and it contains a good deal of what we know as common salt (sodium chloride), there are many other constituents, or ions as chemists call them. The quantities of the most important of these ions in grammes per kilogramme of sea water are as follows: chloride 19·35, sodium 10·76, sulphate 2·71, magnesium 1·29, calcium 0·41, potassium 0·39, bicarbonate 0·14, bromide 0·07, strontium 0·01, boron 0·004 and fluoride 0·001. In addition, there are minute quantities of many other substances, which are present in such small amounts that they are known as trace elements.

Salinity, which is the concentration of all these ions and not just sodium and chloride, is expressed as grammes of ions per kilogramme of sea water. It is always written as parts per thousand (‰) and not as a percentage (%).

In the sea, the salinity usually ranges from 33‰ to 37‰ with an average of 35‰, which is about as salty as a teaspoon of salt in a glass of water. But in the Red Sea it reaches more than 42‰ on the surface and 270‰ at one place on the bottom. In fresh water the salinity is usually less than 0·2‰. When sea water flows into an estuary, it mixes with the fresh water outflow and becomes diluted to form brackish water. Fresh water is lighter than sea water and tends to flow out above the incoming denser salty water. Mixing takes place only between the layers of sea and the river water, where an intermediate layer of brackish water develops. The position and amount of the mixing will depend on the size of the river, and varies considerably from one estuary to another. It will also vary within an estuary, depending on the state of the tide and the flow of water out of the river. The sea will flow further up the estuary during the high-ranging spring tides (see page 26) and also during a dry spell when the river is low.

(e) *Salt-water balance control*

The daily range of salinity experienced by an estuarine inhabitant can be considerable. For example, 12 miles from the sea in the Tamar Estuary, an inhabitant has to survive salinity changes from $25\%_0$ during high water down to $4\%_0$ at low water. Only a few species have been able to adapt to this twice-daily cycle of wide fluctuations in salinity. On the banks of estuaries, the range can be even greater— dropping during a rainstorm or increasing when pools of water evaporate on a hot day.

Most marine animals will die if they are immersed directly in fresh water and similarly most fresh water animals will succumb if dropped straight into sea water, but quite a number of organisms can adapt to slow changes in salinity.

There are several different ways in which marine invertebrate (without vertebrae or a backbone) animals react to salinity changes and control their internal salt-water balance, or *osmoregulate*. Many which live in the open sea, where the salinity remains more or less constant, are known as *conformers*, as the concentration of the salts in their blood is almost *isosmotic* (equal in concentration to the surrounding water).

When the edible mussel feeds by opening its pair of shells under water (see Plate 50), drawing in a current of water and filtering off food particles, the inside tissues are constantly bathed with the surrounding water. Down to $10\%_0$, the blood salts of the mussel are in equal concentration with the surrounding water. But if mussels are kept in water of a salinity below $10\%_0$, they will die. However, when faced with temporary unfavourable conditions, such as exposure at low tide or when the water becomes polluted, the mussel can close its shells, keeping the inside tissue moist. With the shells

6. Lugworm (*Arenicola marina*) burrowing down into sand in a wormery

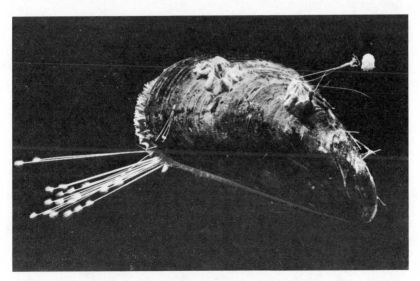

7. Edible mussel (*Mytilus edulis*) attached to inside of aquarium with its byssus. Note the acorn barnacles

closed, a mussel cannot feed, and therefore it will not survive permanently lowered salinities or permanent exposure to air.

Those animals which can regulate the concentration of their blood salts are known as *regulators*. We have already seen that estuarine inhabitants are subject to a wide salinity range. Therefore those species which can regulate their blood salts are more likely to survive and, more important, to be able to breed, in estuaries. There are two kinds of regulators.

The common shore crab (*Carcinus maenas*) (Plate 8), is the most abundant crab in our estuaries and is an example of one kind of regulator. It keeps its blood *hyperosmotic* (higher in concentration) in brackish water and can survive in salinities as low as 6‰. In water saltier than normal sea water, the blood salts increase to the same concentration (isosmotic) as the surrounding water. An example of the second kind of regulator is the shrimp (*Crangon crangon*). It keeps its blood concentration more constant, so that it is *hyposmotic* (lower

8. Shore crab (*Carcinus maenas*) exposed at low water

in concentration) than the surrounding water when the salinity is above $21-23\%_0$; but at lower salinities the blood becomes hyperosmotic.

Fish living and moving through estuaries also have to control their blood salts and their water intake and excretion. The way in which the eel (*Anguilla anguilla*) and the salmon (*Salmo salar*) do this, is described in Chapter 5.

The three-spined stickleback (*Gasterosteus aculeatus*) is a well-known inhabitant of ponds, streams and rivers, so it is perhaps surprising to learn that it migrates into, and lives in, estuaries. Indeed, in northern seas of Britain, it even lives several miles offshore. An interesting recent discovery has been that the number of bony plates along the side of the body of a three-spined stickleback increases as the salinity and the latitude increases. In Belgium, sticklebacks living in brackish water have 20–30 plates on each side of the body, whereas freshwater specimens have only 4–5 plates. In England and France the fish living in fresh water have 3–4 plates between the head and the pelvic fins.

3. *Plants in Estuaries*

In every habitat plants are important because they are the primary producers at the beginning of the food web—they provide food for herbivorous animals, which are themselves eaten by carnivorous animals. An example of a simplified estuarine food web is given in Figure 25.

At the seaward end of an estuary most of the land plants are *maritime*, growing typically near the sea, and are able to tolerate and indeed thrive in regions affected by salt spray. Good examples of a maritime flora grow in the salt-marshes or saltings which are flooded during high spring tides. Moving inland up the estuary the plants become progressively more *riverine*, typical of river banks and marshes.

In the inter-tidal zone, which is covered with water for several hours each day, several *marine* plants grow, including seaweeds which are non-flowering plants and eel-grass, or grass wrack, which is a flowering plant.

(a) *Seaweeds*

Only a few of the seaweeds which occur on rocky shores of the open coast are able to survive living in estuaries. They include the bright green seaweed, *Enteromorpha*, which on rocky shores lives in pools high up the shore—especially where fresh water drains into them. In estuaries it grows over the surface of stable mud flats where its simple, thin fronds may be anything from a few centimetres to 60 cm (2 inches

9. Spiral wrack (*Fucus spiralis*) growing on isolated rocks amongst fine mud at Portishead, on Severn Estuary

to 2 feet) in length. This seaweed is a summer annual which dies off at the end of the season.

Brown seaweeds (they may look olive-green when first exposed) grow in estuaries wherever they can attach themselves to rocks or pier supports. Plate 9 shows clumps of spiral wrack (*Fucus spiralis*) growing on isolated stones projecting from the fine mud at Portishead on the Severn Estuary.

A seaweed has no proper roots; instead, it has an organ—the holdfast—which anchors it to any solid surface. Other brown seaweeds which occur in estuaries are: channelled wrack (*Pelvetia canaliculata*), egg wrack (*Ascophyllum nodosum*), bladder wrack (*Fucus vesiculosus*) and serrated wrack (*Fucus serratus*); but their growth is stunted compared with rocky shore specimens. Horned wrack (*Fucus ceranoides*) is a small brown seaweed which grows only in brackish water.

(b) *Eel-grass*

Three species of eel-grass grow in Britain. Both *Zostera nana* and *Z. hornemanniana* grow on mud flats in estuaries, while the third species, *Z. marina*, prefers the open coast and rarely grows in estuaries. Unlike the brown seaweeds, eel-grass does not require stones for attachment; instead it grows in muddy sand, and its creeping rhizomes often help to stabilise mud banks. The long, green, strap-shaped leaves grow up from a deeply penetrating root system, which makes it difficult to pull up intact. Plate 10 shows eel-grass leaves in a few centimetres of water.

10. Eel-grass (*Zostera* sp.) uncovered at low tide

Early in the 1930s a mysterious disease wiped out the eel-grass beds, which had wide-reaching ecological effects. Firstly, the mud banks on which the eel-grass had grown became eroded. Secondly, the industry which used dried eel-grass for stuffing mattresses collapsed. Thirdly, the numbers of Brent geese—which prefer eel-grass to any other food in their over-wintering grounds in Britain and Europe—were drastically reduced (see page 96).

The eel-grass beds have now re-established themselves but they are still not so extensive as before the disease hit them. Large areas of eel-grass become exposed only at LWST.

(c) *Microscopic organisms*

Also living in the inter-tidal zone are microscopic unicellular (made of one cell) algae, such as diatoms and desmids. Each of these plants is so small (0·015–0·5 mm) that they are barely visible to the naked eye and have to be studied using a microscope. Not all algae (singular alga) are microscopic; for instance, the green and brown seaweeds mentioned on page 38 also belong to this group of lower plants. Most algae live in water—either the sea or fresh water, but some live in damp places such as on tree trunks and walls. The green powdery growth on gates and trees is caused by a terrestrial alga *Pleurococcus* sp.

Sometimes the mud banks lining an estuary that are exposed at low tide gradually develop brown or green streaks. This is the result of very large numbers of microscopic algae moving up to the surface of the mud. It has been found that more than 100,000 *Euglena* occur in 1 square centimetre (sq. cm.) of mud banks along the River Avon at Bristol. By experimenting in a laboratory, scientists have found that light is the main factor which stimulates *Euglena* to move upwards.

Euglena propels itself through water by means of the whip-like flagellum shown in Figure 3 and it also contains chlorophyll. The

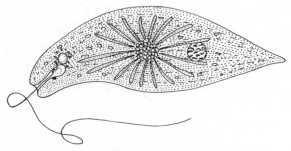

Fig. 3. A flagellated microscopic organism, *Euglena*

ability to move is characteristic of the animal kingdom; whereas the possession of chlorophyll is restricted to the plant kingdom. Therefore *Euglena* has both animal and plant characteristics. Until quite recently it was classified by zoologists as an animal in the group Protozoa, alongside *Amoeba* (which contains no chlorophyll), and by botanists as a plant in the group Thallophyta. Now a new major kingdom—the Protista—has been created to group together unicellular microscopic organisms in general whether they do or do not possess chlorophyll, or can or cannot move. It is in this new kingdom that *Euglena* is now placed.

Euglena, because it contains the green pigment chlorophyll, is able in sunlight to carry out the process of building up sugars from water and carbon dioxide, which is known as photosynthesis. Chlorophyll is essential for photosynthesis, but not all plants which are able to photosynthesise appear green: for example, in brown and red seaweeds other pigments mask the green of the chlorophyll. However, regardless of their colour, all photosynthetic plants can be referred to as *manufacturers* or *producers*; in contrast to the animals which feed on them, which can be called *consumers*.

Diatoms are important producers on mud flats, where they are fed on by protozoans, flatworms, round worms, ostracods (mussel shrimps), the ragworm (*Nereis* sp.) (Plates 27 and 28) and the snail (*Hydrobia ulvae*) (Plate 26 and Figure 17). Each diatom consists of two valves which are made of silica. One valve overlaps the other so that the diatom superficially resembles a beautifully sculptured pill box. Figure 4 is a drawing of a highly magnified diatom.

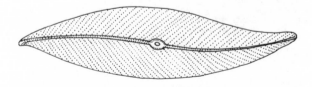

Fig. 4. An estuarine diatom, *Pleurosigma aestuarii*

(d) *Salt marsh plants*

A salt marsh community of flowering plants typically develops in the uppermost tidal reaches of a sheltered estuary or a tidal creek, where there are few waves or currents. Most of the plants in this community, which stretches from HWNT to HWST, are covered only spasmodically by salt or brackish water. Plants which are adapted for survival in a salt laden atmosphere, or submerged in sea water, are known as *halophytes*.

Only a few salt marsh plants are annuals, such as glasswort or marsh samphire (*Salicornia europaea*) and annual seablite (*Suaeda maritima*), which live on the unstable sand and mud along the seaward edge of the marshes. The majority of salt marsh plants are perennials and live at a slightly higher level on more stable ground. Many of these plants are long-lived; for example in Norfolk, individual plants

11. Glasswort or marsh samphire (*Salicornia europaea*)

of sea lavender (*Limonium vulgare*) are estimated to be more than 40 years old.

A characteristic feature of salt marshes is that the plants tend to grow in zones. There are a few species which always begin to colonise bare mud, but not every species occurs in every salt marsh.

In the middle reaches of an estuary glasswort first colonises either bare mud or mud banks, where it is submerged for a few hours each day. Plate 11 shows the fleshy segments which help to conserve water when the plants become exposed. The tiny yellow-green flowers are produced in late summer.

The initial colonisation by individual plants slows down the water current so that more of the mud carried in suspension settles out and thereby raises the level of the bank. Because glasswort has shallow roots it is unable to gain a foothold in places where the currents are strong. The ash which is left after burning glasswort contains soda which was used in glass making.

Annual seablite which often grows alongside glasswort is also a

Fig. 5. Annual seablite (*Suaeda maritima*) in flower

Fig. 6. Flowering sea aster (*Aster tripolium*)

fleshy plant. Its colour and general habit are very variable: the leaves may be green or red and the plant can be erect or creeping. The erect form is illustrated in Figure 5. This seablite should not be confused with perennial shrubby seablite (*Suaeda fruticosa*) which grows on shingle banks above HWST.

Also often growing with glasswort and seablite are sea manna grass (*Puccinellia maritima*) and sea aster (*Aster tripolium*). The daisy-like, purple flowers with yellow centres of the sea aster tower above most of the other salt marsh plants on their 60–100 cm (2–3 feet) long stalks. Sea aster, which is illustrated in Figure 6, is not by any means confined to salt marshes, and it can often be seen growing on cliffs by the sea.

Unlike glasswort, rice-grass or cord-grass (*Spartina townsendii*) will colonise bare mud (Plate 12) in places with a current. This

12. Cord grass (*Spartina townsendii*) colonising bare mud in Sussex

grass, which was first recorded from Southampton Water in 1870, is a natural hybrid between an American species (*S. alternifolia*) and the native (*S. maritima*). A hybrid is the offspring which results from parents of two different species and, typically in plants, grows more vigorously than either of its parents. The rice-grass hybrid (Figure 7) is unusual in that it produces seeds which are fertile. From the initial locality, it has spread extensively around the Southampton and Poole Harbour area.

This vigorously-growing perennial is much more effective at trapping silt and raising the soil level than glasswort. For this reason, it has been introduced to many areas to assist in land reclamation. No other salt marsh plant in Britain is so successful at building up and claiming land from the sea.

In the middle region of the marsh are two easily recognisable plants. The smaller thrift or sea pink (*Armeria maritima*) with its globular pink flowers is an equally common sight on sea cliffs. Whereas the 30-cm (1-foot) tall sea lavender is restricted to salt

Fig. 7. Cord grass (*Spartina townsendii*) showing flowering spike

Fig. 8. Sea lavender (*Limonium vulgare*) flowering

marshes. Figure 8 shows the way a mass of tiny flowers crowd together in a sea lavender head. In some places sea lavender grows so well that the whole of the middle salt marsh appears as a sheet of pale mauve in July.

Salt pans are a common feature of the middle marsh. Formed by the blockage of small drainage channels, the pans trap sea water when a high tide floods the marsh. When the water in the pans evaporates it leaves bare mud covered with salt crystals. Around the edge of the pans, where the salinity is particularly high, sea plantain (*Plantago maritima*) and sea arrow-grass (*Triglochin maritima*) may not produce flowers—instead all their energy goes towards vegetative reproduction.

Where drainage channels run through the middle marsh they are bordered by grey-green clumps of sea purslane (*Halimione portulacoides*) (Figure 9). Here the channel margins become built up by material carried with the incoming tide, until they lie well above the water course. Therefore the banks themselves are well-drained—an essential factor for the good growth of sea purslane. Although this plant does not have colourful flowers like thrift, sea aster or sea

Fig. 9. Sea purslane
(*Halimione portulacoides*)

lavender, it is instantly recognisable throughout the year, as a greyish band bordering creeks as shown in Plate 13. When the marsh itself becomes drained, then sea purslane will begin to invade out from the creeks.

13. Sea purslane (*Halimione portulacoides*) growing on raised ground along margins of drainage channels

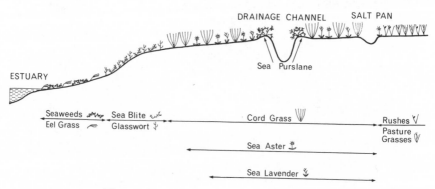

Fig. 10. Profile across generalised salt marsh

Finally, in the upper regions of the marsh, where sea rush (*Juncus maritimus*) and various grasses, including red fescue grass (*Festuca rubra*), begin to grow, sheep and cattle come down to graze. Figure 10 shows a generalised diagram of the zonation of the most conspicuous estuarine plants, from low tide level to the top of the salt marsh at HWST.

4. *Animal Residents*

Because an estuary is a place where fresh water and the sea meet and become mixed, it is a habitat in which relatively few species of animals have adapted to survive and live as permanent residents in the upper reaches. But, as we shall see, those species which have adapted do not face such great competition as the marine inhabitants of the open coast or the freshwater inhabitants of rivers. Therefore true estuarine species are often present in very large numbers and high densities.

The resident animals can be divided into three distinct groups. There are the marine species which have moved up from the sea, the freshwater species which have penetrated down from the river and

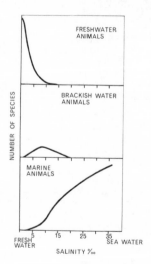

Fig. 11. Relative numbers of freshwater, brackish water and marine species along the length of an estuary

in a small region in the middle are the true estuarine or brackish water animals. Figure 11 shows the proportion of species within each of these groups along the length of the estuary. As would be expected, there are most marine species at the seaward end of the estuary and most freshwater species at the far end of the estuary. In the middle of the estuary few species remain from these two groups, and the true brackish species occur.

MARINE ANIMALS

Firstly, let us take the marine species, and especially those which can be found living in the inter-tidal zone which becomes exposed at low water. The three main factors which limit their distribution in estuaries are: salinity, the type of bottom and the length of exposure during low water. For instance, mussels will live only where they can attach themselves to a solid substrate and where the salinity does not fall below 4‰. Because mussels filter-feed by sieving tiny particles from the water, they can feed only when they are submerged. Therefore the lower down the shore mussels live, the longer they are covered during each tide and so the longer they can feed.

The marine inter-tidal animals can be further subdivided into those that move and live on the surface of the shore (the epifauna) and those that live in burrows (the infauna). The latter are mainly worms and bivalve molluscs.

(a) *Crustaceans*

A common epifaunal animal widespread in estuaries is the shore crab, illustrated in Plate 8. Crabs, together with lobsters, prawns and shrimps, belong to a group of Crustaceans called decapods (deca = ten, pod = foot), which have ten limbs—a pair of pincers and four pairs of walking legs. True crabs, including the shore crabs, have a tiny flap-like abdomen which is tucked beneath the body. The sex of a crab can be determined by looking at the shape of this flap (be careful that you hold a crab by the back edge of the shell where the pincers cannot reach you!)—females have a broad flap with seven segments, whereas males have a narrow five-segmented flap.

Regardless of its colour, which may be green, orange or mottled brown, the shore crab can always be recognized by the five sharp teeth on either side of the eyes on the edge of the shell. Although it can burrow down into sand, the shore crab prefers shores with stones or seaweeds for cover.

This crab is extremely hardy—tolerating salinities down to 6‰ and feeding both as a predator and a scavenger. It has distinct patterns of activity—being most active during high tides at night. In the summer, shore crabs tend to move upshore with the incoming tide and remain there when it ebbs back. Whereas when the temperature drops in winter, they either tend to move back down the shore with the ebbing tide, or if it gets very cold, they may not move up the shore at all. In some estuaries *Carcinus* moves out towards the sea in winter, but female crabs with eggs tend to stay in the seaward end of the estuary until the larvae hatch. When crabs are carrying their eggs they are known as 'being in berry'. A berried female may be confused

14. Underside of female shore crab (*Carcinus maenas*) showing egg mass

with a crab which has been parasitised by the sac barnacle (*Sacculina carcini*). Both berried crabs and parasitised crabs have a large sac-like growth under their abdominal flap, but the parasite's eggs are enclosed in a yellow or orange sac, whereas the crab eggs are quite separate and not enclosed by a membrane (Plate 14).

Crab eggs take several weeks to hatch into tiny zoeae larvae which live and feed as part of the zooplankton (animal plankton). The zoeae have a long spine on the head and a large backwardly pointing dorsal spine. The first-stage zoea, which is 1·4 mm, feeds and moults several times until it reaches the 3·2 mm fourth-stage zoea. This changes into the megalopa stage which eventually settles on the bottom and metamorphoses into a small crab.

Carcinus lives for 3–4 years, sometimes reaching a size of 90–100 mm (4 inches) across the carapace, although the largest crabs are found on the open coast and not in estuaries. Crabs have a hard outer exoskeleton and so this must be shed before they can grow bigger. A crab sheds its old carapace by walking out backwards through a slit which develops across the back edge of the carapace.

You may be lucky and find a complete discarded carapace lying on the shore, but usually the legs will have dropped off so that only the main part is left. If the cast is complete you will see that even the gills inside the carapace are shed. The crab when it emerges has a soft shell, and so it is particularly vulnerable to predators—including gulls. So at this time, more than any other, crabs need the protective covering of seaweeds and stones to hide under during low water.

Other crustaceans found in estuaries include shrimps and prawns. The estuarine prawn (*Palaemonetes varians*) is one typical example. The edible brown shrimp (*Crangon crangon = C. vulgaris*) is so called because it turns brownish-pink on boiling. The pink shrimp is in fact a small prawn. Shrimps have a much more flattened body than prawns. Also they have a very short forwardly projecting rostrum and only one pair of appendages with pincers. Shrimps frequent sandy or muddy areas where they spend the day buried in the sand, coming out at night to feed. Their mottled grey-brown colouring makes them difficult to spot on the sand, as can be seen in Plate 15.

Shrimps will feed on a variety of food, from green plants to smaller

15. Shrimp (*Crangon crangon*) moving over bottom of aquarium

crustaceans, worms—including large ragworms (*Nereis* sp.) and molluscs. They either crawl over the sand on their last two pairs of legs, or else they can swim through the water—but not so efficiently as prawns.

In winter, shrimps move down estuaries and out to sea. The females seem able to tolerate estuarine water better than the males, as they are the first to return in the Spring and the last to leave in Winter. The females also live longer (4–5 years) than the males (3 years). Usually only one brood is produced in the estuary, whereas two broods are produced in the sea. In the Severn Estuary shrimps breed from March to June. The eggs are carried by the females beneath their tail. Like crabs, the eggs hatch into planktonic larvae, which moult several times before settling on the bottom as small shrimps.

Shrimps are caught commercially in Morecambe Bay and on the Kent and Essex coasts, usually in inshore boats with trawls. The method used at Stolford in Bridgwater Bay of catching them during the ebbing tide in staked nets has been in operation since before the Doomsday Book. Shrimps can be found by raking the sand surface.

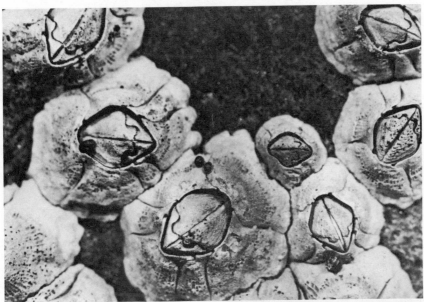

16. Acorn barnacles
(*Balanus balanoides*)
exposed at low water

17. Acorn barnacle
(*Balanus*) with
extended cirri,
feeding under water

This disturbs them so they come to the surface, where they can be caught by hand.

Barnacles, which encrust rocks on the shore, may look more like molluscs, but their free-swimming larvae show that they are distinctly crustaceans. *Elminius modestus* is a barnacle which reached European waters from Australia during the Second World War. It was first reported in Britain from Chichester Harbour and the Thames Estuary in 1945, since when it has spread around the coast and even across to Ireland. *Elminius* has four outer limey plates, while the other barnacles found in estuaries, such as *Balanus balanoides*, have six outer plates (see Plate 16). *Elminius* is more successful at spreading up estuaries than *Balanus* because it can tolerate dilute sea water better and it also has a longer breeding season.

Barnacles feed only when submerged; the small plates which cover over the top, open so that the feeding limbs (cirri) emerge to comb the water (Plate 17) for minute food particles.

Once the last larval stage (the cypris) has settled and changed into a small barnacle, it is fixed for life. Barnacles are hermaphrodite animals; in other words an individual is both male and female, but it cannot fertilise itself. Each barnacle has to be cross-fertilised by another barnacle. Because barnacles cannot move around, it is important that they settle down close to a potential mate. This they do by being attracted to a chemical substance produced by the older barnacles. So here is the reason why barnacles occur in groups or clusters and why you are unlikely to see a solitary barnacle. Animals which group together are called *gregarious*.

As with all animals which produce larval stages, the distribution of a barnacle species up an estuary depends not only on the adults being able to survive in lower salinities, but also the larval stages.

Another group of crustaceans found in estuaries are the sand-hoppers or Amphipods (amphi = two kinds, pod = foot). These include several species of *Gammarus*, whose bodies are flattened from side to side. They move by wriggling on their side, and when exposed they scuttle under cover of seaweed or stones. Each species shows a distinct salinity range, so that as the water becomes less salty, one species gradually replaces another, with some overlapping. Passing into an estuary from the sea, the first species to be found is *Gammarus locusta*, which lives along the coast in shallow water amongst seaweeds as well as penetrating up the mouth of estuaries. *G. zaddachi* occurs at the head of estuaries up to any tributaries which still have a tidal rise and fall. *G. salinus* lives in the mid-estuary, overlapping with *G. locusta* at the seaward end and *G. zaddachi* at the river end of its range. The true brackish water species *G. duebeni* is described and illustrated on page 74.

(b) *Molluscs*

We will now leave the crustaceans and look at some familiar molluscs. Beds of blue-black edible mussels are a common sight on many rocky shores (Plate 18) and, wherever they can attach themselves to a solid support, they will be found in estuaries where the salinity is greater than 4‰. Some of the best commercial mussel beds are at

18. A tightly packed bed of edible mussels (*Mytilus edulis*)

mouths of estuaries; especially Conway Bay, Morecambe Bay and the Wash.

To prevent themselves from being washed away, mussels produce a mass of tough brownish threads known as the byssus. The threads originate as a sticky substance produced by a gland inside the reddish-brown foot. When the foot is pushed out from between the shells on to the rock face, a buoy or an aquarium wall, a fluid runs along a groove in the foot and hardens on contact with sea water. Eventually the mussel becomes attached by many of these threads diverging out from inside it, as shown in Plate 7.

Each mussel has a pair of shells or valves which distinguish it as a

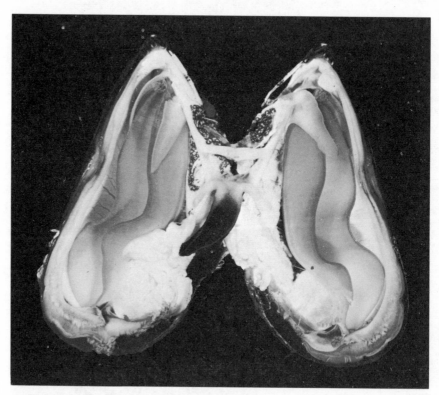

19. Edible mussel (*Mytilus edulis*) opened up under water to show gills inside each valve

bivalve mollusc in contrast with winkles and whelks which are *univalve* molluscs. When exposed to the air, mussels close their valves to prevent their insides from drying out. Like barnacles, mussels feed only when they are submerged in sea water. Plate 50 shows a pair of mussels with open valves feeding under water in an aquarium. In between each pair of valves are two siphons. Water is drawn into the mussel through the frilly-edged siphon and passed out through the smooth-edged siphon. Notice the plain outgoing (exhalent) siphon is the smaller of the two. Can you think what is the reason for this? The answer is given on page 116 with the description of the mussel feeding experiment. The water is drawn into the mussel by tiny hairs (cilia) on the surface of the orange gills beating and creating a current. Plate 19 shows how these gills fill most of the mussel's inside. The gills extract oxygen from the water and also filter out the minute plant plankton and organic detritus from the water on which the mussel feeds. So like barnacles, mussels are called *filter-feeders*.

One word of warning here: while mussels are excellent to eat, they should never be collected for eating unless you are certain the water is not polluted in any way.

Mussels breed by shedding the sex cells (eggs and sperm) into the water. When an egg is fertilised by a sperm it develops into a larva known as a *veliger*, which lives for several weeks as part of the plankton. Then when it can both swim and crawl, it becomes known as a *periveliger* and settles. The most extensive mussel beds are formed below low water, where the animals can feed almost continuously. Only a few mussels settle above mid-tide level.

The native oyster (*Ostrea edulis*) is another bivalve which can live in estuaries. Extensive oyster beds used to exist in the mouth of the Thames Estuary, but severe winters, pollution and the invasion of oyster pests have ruined several productive oyster beds on the east coast. This is discussed in more detail on page 103.

Two species of winkles (or periwinkles), which occur on rocky shores, penetrate up estuaries. These are the 1 cm ($\frac{2}{5}$ inch) rough winkle (*Littorina saxatilis*) (Plate 20) which has a ribbed shell, and the 2·5 cm (1 inch) brownish edible winkle (*L. littorea*) (Plate 21). The rough winkle is able to withstand both a lower salinity (down to

20. Rough periwinkles
(*Littorina saxatilis*)
at low tide

21. Edible periwinkles
(*Littorina littorea*)

8‰) than the edible winkle (down to 10‰) and drying for longer periods. Both species have an operculum which seals off the shell opening at low water. The edible winkle is often very abundant in salt marsh creeks.

Each winkle breeds in a different way. Like most marine snails, the edible winkle lays eggs, which hatch into veliger larvae, whereas the rough periwinkle broods its eggs and the young are born alive. Animals which do not lay eggs but give birth to live young are known as *viviparous*.

So far, we have been looking at marine animals which live on, and move over, the shore of estuaries. Now we will turn our attention to the animals which burrow into the mud and sand. These animals include mainly worms and bivalve molluscs.

(c) *The Lugworm*
A worm which is familiar to all sea anglers is the lugworm, which is used as bait. Worm casts on the shore (Plate 22) mark the position of

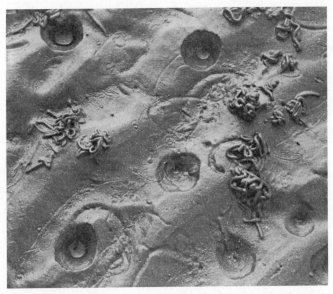

22. Casts and depressions made by feeding lugworms (*Arenicola marina*)

23. Complete lugworm (*Arenicola marina*) dug out from its burrow

the tail end of a lugworm's burrow. You will have to dig down 20–30 cm (9–12 inches) (a large garden fork is easier than a spade) to find a lugworm, which never lies on the surface of the sand. When you have dug one out, wash the mud from the worm so you can see its main features as illustrated in Plate 23. The body of an adult worm is about as thick as a pencil. It is segmented and there is a rough circular proboscis which can be pushed out or withdrawn into the mouth. On each side of the middle region are 13 pairs of red feathery gills. This colour is due to the red pigment haemoglobin occurring in the blood.

Figure 12 shows a lugworm lying in its U-shaped burrow in a wormery. Wormeries are used in schools for observing the way earthworms burrow, but they are also ideal for watching lugworms in action. A wormery is a very narrow container with a glass front and back. Fill it two-thirds full of the mud or sand collected from where the lugworms occur and then top it with sea water.

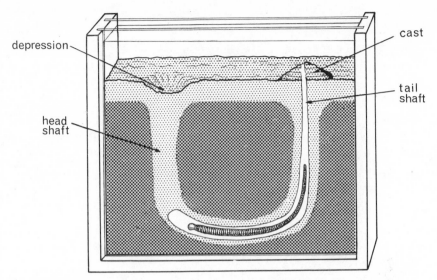

depression

cast

tail shaft

head shaft

Fig. 12. Lugworm (*Arenicola marina*) in wormery, showing its cast and depression at the surface

A lugworm remains in its tube to feed. It swallows the sand nearest its head, so more sand sinks down the head shaft and so forms the surface depression. Every 45 minutes it backs up the tail shaft to defaecate and so adds to the cast at the surface. *Arenicola* has to swallow sand for several hours each day in order to extract enough detritus as food.

At Whitstable in the Thames Estuary, lugworms spawn during the last fortnight in October, especially during the neap tides. The eggs and sperm are released on to the surface of the beach where they are mixed together by the incoming tide. The eggs hatch into larvae which live on the bottom, and are not free-living amongst the plankton, like those of most other shore animals (see mussel, p. 59).

The ragworm (*Nereis diversicolor*) is another very common worm of estuaries and is described in the section on Brackish Water Animals on page 71.

(d) *Burrowing bivalves*

Living in the mud banks are a variety of bivalves—some small, some large. Ribbed shells of the edible cockle (*Cerastoderma = Cardium edule*) (Figure 13) are often washed up on shores. *C. edule* will live in estuaries down to a salinity of 18‰, whereas *C. larmarcki* can tolerate salinities as low as 5‰. Cockles, which bury themselves just below the surface, can be collected by raking. Their siphons, which are longer than those of mussels, can be extended up to the surface. Water carrying oxygen and food particles is drawn in through the inhalent

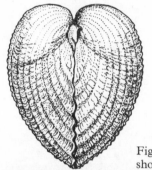

Fig. 13. Edible cockle (*Cerastoderma edule*) edge-on showing the interlocking of the two valves

24. Cockle (*Cerastoderma edule*) feeding under water, showing its two siphons emerging from between the valves

siphon, and expelled through the exhalent siphon, together with the waste products. Plate 24 shows a cockle under water with its siphons projecting.

The 6-cm (2½-inch) long, pale yellowish, peppery furrow shell (*Scrobicularia plana*) lives much deeper down, as its inhalent siphon can extend as much as 28 cm (11 inches) up to the surface. *Scrobicularia* feeds by using the inhalent siphon rather like a vacuum cleaner to suck up surface detritus over a circular area (see Figure 14).

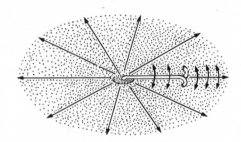

Fig. 14. Diagram of the feeding movements made by the inhalent siphon of the peppery furrow shell (*Scrobicularia plana*)

Scrobicularia feeds during low tide for as long as it is covered with water. At high tide it withdraws the siphon and feeds inside the mouth of the burrow, so the siphon cannot be seen and eaten by crabs or fish.

Animals which feed on the surface of mud or sand, rather than on particles suspended in the water, are known as *deposit* feeders. *Scrobicularia* can live in the zone of black bad-smelling mud, which lacks oxygen, because it feeds and draws in water from the surface. At this level, deep in the mud, it avoids competition for burrow space with other shallower-dwelling species. So long as it is not subjected to prolonged low temperature, *Scrobicularia* may live for as long as 18 years. During the severe 1962/3 Winter a great proportion of the British populations died.

Other deposit-feeding bivalve molluscs found in estuaries are the Baltic tellin (*Macoma balthica*) and the thin tellin (*Tellina tenuis*). The 2·5-cm (1-inch) long Baltic tellin is smaller than the peppery furrow shell, and it does not burrow so deeply; however, it can tolerate the cold much better. Where both species occur in the same area, they may compete to the extent that one species dominates the other. For instance, in the Gwendraeth Estuary, 500–1024 *Scrobicularia* were found with 0–10 *Macoma* per square metre, whereas in the Mersey Estuary the positions were reversed. Here there were no *Scrobicularia* and 2,000–5,900 of *Macoma* per square metre. The shape of a *Macoma* shell is illustrated in Figure 15a. The colour is very variable, either white, yellow, pink or purple. It gets its common name from the large numbers which live in the Baltic Sea.

The 2-cm ($\frac{4}{5}$-inch) long, glossy-shelled thin tellin (Figure 15b) prefers coarser deposits and higher salinities than either *Scrobicularia* or *Macoma*. Unlike *Scrobicularia*, which lies on one end (see Figure 24), *Tellina* lies on its side, but it also extends a long siphon up to the surface. Dense concentrations of *Tellina* become spaced out evenly in the sand because the bivalves do not like their siphons to touch when they are feeding.

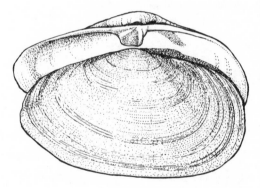

Fig. 15a. One valve of the Baltic
tellin (*Macoma balthica*)
b. One valve of the thin
tellin (*Tellina tenuis*)

Fig. 16. Pair of valves of the sand gaper (*Mya arenaria*)

The sand gaper or soft-shelled clam (*Mya arenaria*) (Figure 16) with its large (10·5-cm ($4\frac{1}{5}$-inch) long) oval shells, is unmistakable. The valves gape permanently, because the massive siphons always protrude from the shell. As it grows bigger, it burrows deeper. If a gaper is dug up and left on the beach, it is unable to burrow down again. This gaper is farmed in coastal waters and estuaries in America.

The hard shell clam or quahog (*Venus* [= *Mercenaria*] *mercenaria*) has a large, rounded shell with a distinct beak. It is also eaten in America, and there have been several unsuccessful attempts to introduce it to the Dee (Cheshire) and Mersey Estuaries. The colonies which exist today, in Southampton Water and Portsmouth Harbour, possibly originated from kitchen waste thrown overboard from trans-Atlantic liners.

(e) *Fishes*

Many marine fish move in and out of the mouth of an estuary, but only a few penetrate and feed for long periods within the estuary, such as the flounder (*Platichthys flesus*), the grey mullet (*Crenimugil labrosus* = *Mugil chelo*) and the common goby (*Pomatoschistus* [= *Gobius*] *microps*).

25. Flounder (*Platichthys flesus*) swimming down on to sandy bottom of an aquarium

The flounder is the only British flat fish which can move up estuaries and live for a short time in fresh water. Flounders do not grow quite so large as plaice, but they can reach a length of about 51 cm (17 inches). The upper side is usually mottled brown (with no obvious orange spots like a plaice) and the underside is white. The sides of the body are fringed with a fin border. Like all true flat fish, when resting they lie on one side (usually the left side for flounders) and not on their belly. Flounders can also swim actively through the water, as Plate 25 shows.

Next time you see a complete flat fish, have a look at the head. You will see the position of the mouth and eyes is twisted. When the larva hatches from an egg, it looks much like any other fish larvae, with an eye on either side of the mouth. But when it metamorphoses from the planktonic larval stage into a bottom-living fish, the lower eye moves up so that both eyes come to lie on the upper side. Therefore when a flounder buries itself, it can keep a pair of watchful eyes poking out of the sand.

Flounders spend some months feeding in estuaries, returning to the sea in the Spring to breed. Their freshwater diet includes freshwater snails, insect larvae and crustaceans. In the estuary they feed on cockles, Baltic tellins, young shore crabs, shrimps, opossum shrimps, *Corophium* and common gobies.

The grey or thick-lipped mullet also moves into estuaries to feed and returns to the sea to breed. It is usually the immature fish which can be seen in shoals entering estuaries in southern Britain. The fish have a dark grey-green back and silvery sides, with six to seven faint grey lines running along each side from the head to the tail.

Grey mullet have no teeth and they browse mainly on diatoms and green algae. They often come into harbours to feed on green algae growing on piers and on microscopic algae in muddy bottoms, straining food from the mud by using the fine comb-like fringes on their lips. Sometimes they eat mollusc larvae and small crustaceans. Grey mullet grow to a length of about 50 cm (18 inches).

The common goby is both the most numerous goby between the tide marks of sandy and muddy shores, and the most abundant fish in British estuaries. Like all gobies, it has two separate dorsal fins, and the pelvic fins are fused to form a sucker on the underside. This sucker is used to attach the fish to stones in fairly calm water.

This goby will penetrate up into the upper reaches of an estuary in Summer, but it returns to the sea to breed. Its food is very variable —when in fresh water it competes with the minnow for midge (chironomid) larvae, but in the estuary it feeds mainly on small crustaceans, and on shrimps.

The 7-cm ($2\frac{3}{4}$-inch) long common goby spawns during April to August. The eggs are laid underneath an empty bivalve shell— especially a sand gaper or a cockle shell. If the shell is lying inside uppermost, the male goby pushes it over. Then he drives sand from beneath the shell by creating a strong current. When the space beneath the shell is big enough, he moves in and turns round so that his head points outwards. He then develops his darker breeding dress—with blue edges to the pectoral and ventral fins and a blue iris to the eye.

When he succeeds in attracting a ripe female to his 'nest', she enters and turns upside down so that the eggs are laid in batches on the underside of the shell. After each batch is laid, it is fertilised by the male. Once she has finished laying, the female leaves the nest, which is guarded over and aerated by the male goby. If the male is taken away from the nest, other male gobies eat the eggs.

ESTUARINE OR BRACKISH WATER ANIMALS

This section includes the typical estuarine species which regularly occur in salinities below 30‰, and which do not normally live either in the sea or in fresh water.

If you walk out over the surface of estuarine mud flats, the animal you cannot fail to see—even though it is only 6 mm ($\frac{1}{4}$ inch) long—is the snail called *Hydrobia*. Thomas Pennant, the eighteenth-century naturalist, first described it as being 'the size of a grain of wheat'. *Hydrobia* is one of the most abundant animals of the mud flats; densities of 42,000 per square metre of *H. ulvae* occur in the Clyde Estuary, and Plate 26 shows a group exposed on the mud surface in Sussex.

26. A group of *Hydrobia ulvae* snails clustered together on the mud at low tide

The three different species of *Hydrobia* which occur in estuaries are very difficult to identify with certainty. The usual characters of shell shape and colouration are inadequate and the internal parts have to be examined as well.

The behaviour of *Hydrobia* throughout the tidal cycle, has been studied in detail at Whitstable on the Thames Estuary. When first exposed, the *Hydrobia* snails crawl over the mud browsing on detritus and diatoms. Then they burrow down into the mud, and emerge just before the incoming tide reaches them. Each snail forms a mucous raft which both keeps it afloat and also acts as a food net by trapping plankton. It stays afloat and is carried back down to its original level by the ebbing tide, until it breaks away from the surface film, withdraws into its shell and sinks down on to the mud to start the cycle again. Figure 17 shows the underside of *Hydrobia* when feeding on the surface film. Notice that the left tentacle is both thicker and hairier than the right one.

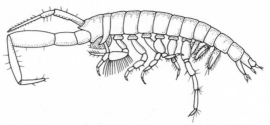

Fig. 17. *Hydrobia ulvae* snail showing the way it swims and feeds on the surface film

Fig. 18. Brackish water amphipod, *Corophium volutator*

Hydrobia lays its eggs in gelatinous capsules which are often attached to another *Hydrobia* snail. Like several other molluscs previously described, the eggs hatch into planktonic veliger larvae.

Corophium volutator, illustrated in Figure 18, is a 1-cm ($\frac{2}{5}$-inch) long amphipod typically associated with estuaries—often occurring in very high densities. In the Tamar Estuary 11,000 per square metre have been recorded, while 63,000 young per square metre have been found in the Dovey Estuary. Together with *Hydrobia*, it is one of the most abundant animals in estuarine mud banks, but it is found neither in clean sand nor in polluted places.

Corophium uses its very long pair of second antennae for pulling itself over the mud in a looping fashion. When the mud banks are first uncovered, both the animals and their tracks can be seen on the surface, but soon the animals burrow down into their U-shaped burrows. While *Corophium* can survive in salinities of 2–36‰, it needs a salinity of at least 5‰ to grow and moult, and more than 7·5‰ to breed. Females carry their eggs in a brood pouch until they hatch.

Nereis diversicolor is the ragworm abundant in estuarine muds. This estuarine worm penetrates much further up estuaries than the lugworms because it is able to survive much lower salinities. Although it can tolerate a salinity as low as 1‰ it cannot live or breed in fresh water.

The 8–10 cm (3–4 inch) long body of this yellow-brown ragworm is divided into 90–120 obvious segments. It has a very conspicuous red blood vessel running along the length of its back. At the front end

27. Enlarged head of adult ragworm (*Nereis* sp.) showing black chitinous jaws and tentacles
28. Juvenile ragworm (*Nereis diversicolor*) emerging to feed on the mud surface. Portishead, Severn Estuary

are paired feelers and a retractile proboscis ending in a pair of black chitinous jaws (Plate 27). If you dig up ragworms for bait be careful not to squeeze them, because this will push out the jaws, which can give you a painful nip.

The ragworm lives in a slime-lined burrow in the mud. Unlike the lugworm, it emerges to feed (Plate 28), so that the burrow entrance often becomes marked by a series of radiating tracks. The ragworm is both a scavenger—eating detritus and any dead or dying animals— and a predator—eating small crustaceans.

In the south of England, ragworms spawn in February when the temperature reaches 5°C. The female worms die after spawning as the eggs are shed by their bodies splitting. The eggs are fertilised by sperm released by the males and hatch into larvae which stay on the bottom, so they do not get swept out to sea.

Mysids, commonly known as opossum shrimps, are not true shrimps. They spend much time swimming in mid-water and so are planktonic. They feed mostly by filtering minute plants (phytoplankton) and animals (zooplankton), but occasionally they may capture individual larger planktonic animals, or scavenge on even larger crustaceans. Female opossum shrimps carry eggs and young in a brood pouch formed by the bases of the hind thoracic limbs.

Neomysis integer, illustrated in Figure 19, is a typically estuarine species occurring from the mouth to the head of estuaries in well-

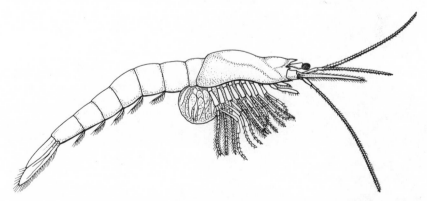

Fig. 19. An opossum shrimp, *Neomysis integer*— a female with brood pouch

aerated water. When the tide rises, large numbers of these mysids may gather together along the water's edge. *Neomysis* is not found in estuarine waters which are polluted or lack oxygen. It breeds throughout the year, but the size of the broods are smaller in Winter (10–25) than in Summer (20–50).

Praunus flexuosus is a larger mysid (25 mm) (1 inch) which lives in brackish waters—often associated with *Neomysis*. It feeds on small crustaceans, and also pieces of leaves and seeds washed or blown from the land. In Summer, *Praunus* swarms along the banks of the Tamar—especially at Saltash.

Gammarus duebeni (Figure 20) is the true brackish water shrimp of estuaries, being able to withstand a wide salinity range. On the mainland of Britain it does not penetrate up into fresh water, because it cannot compete with *G. pulex*, which has a higher reproduction rate. In Ireland *G. pulex* does not occur naturally, and *G. duebeni* is the freshwater species. In *G. duebeni* the sex of the young varies with the water temperature: males being produced below 5°C, females at about 6°C and either sex if the temperature is between 5–6°C.

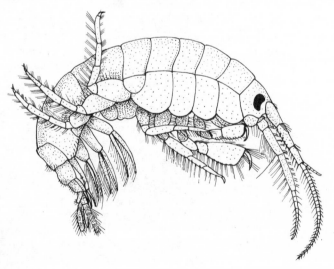

Fig. 20. Brackish water shrimp, *Gammarus duebeni*

Two other brackish water species are a colonial animal, *Cordylophora*, and the flatworm *Procerodes* (= *Gunda*) *ulvae*. *Cordylophora* is related to the tiny freshwater Hydra which has a ring of tentacles surrounding the mouth at the end of the sac-like body known as a polyp. Instead of having a single polyp, *Cordylophora* has many polyps—rather like miniature sea anemones—joined together on a stalk to form a colony. The size of the *Cordylophora* colony is directly related to the water temperature and the salinity. In high temperatures or in fresh water the colony grows shorter than in low temperatures or when the salinity is above 20‰. *Cordylophora* grows best in a salinity of 15‰. *Procerodes* lives in small streams which run down through the intertidal zone.

FRESHWATER ANIMALS

We now come to the last group of aquatic animals which reside in estuaries. The majority of freshwater species are stopped from moving down an estuary by quite small salinity increases and relatively few species can tolerate even slightly brackish water.

Near the head of estuaries—especially in polluted regions—the mud banks are inhabited by an abundance of sludge worms, *Tubifex* sp. These aquatic worms are close relatives of earthworms. The common name for *Tubifex* refers to another habitat where they abound—the filter beds of sewage farms.

Tubifex will tolerate salinities up to 5‰. The worms can be so numerous in the mud flats of the Thames Estuary that at low water the banks appear quite red. Each worm lives head-down in a chimney-like tube built up from the muddy bottom. The tail end, which pokes out of the top of the tube, beats to and fro, driving a current of water towards the head. If the worm is disturbed, then it withdraws its tail down into the tube.

Tubifex is tolerant of both low oxygen conditions and chemical pollutants. In these habitats, which are unfavourable to other species, its numbers can increase as they are unchecked by competitors or predators. *Tubifex* is quite capable of living in well-oxygenated water, but there it has to compete with many other species.

Tubifex has blood rich in haemoglobin, and is highly efficient at extracting what little oxygen there is in the water. Like earthworms, *Tubifex* lays eggs in cocoons, from which small worms hatch.

When sludge worms are kept in water with no mud they tend to group themselves into a balled mass. It is these writhing masses which are sold in pet shops as live fish food. Mud with the worms in it is collected from river banks and put on to strips of hessian placed over tubs of clean water. The worms wriggle through the hessian and drop into the tubs below.

The pale brown freshwater shrimp (*Gammarus pulex*) (Plate 29) is yet another *Gammarus* species which occurs in estuaries. As the common name suggests, it normally lives higher up than *G. duebeni*, but the two species can overlap. *G. pulex* reproduces more efficiently in fresh water than *G. duebeni*, and so is better adapted to live there. *G. pulex* is not a true shrimp. It is very abundant in running fresh water, especially streams and rivers, where it often shelters beneath stones.

29. Freshwater shrimp (*Gammarus pulex*) under water

In Spring and Summer when the female carries eggs or young in her brood pouch, she is carried around in tandem by the male. The young hatch directly from the egg, without any larval stage.

The water louse or hog slater (*Asellus aquaticus*) (Plate 30) is a freshwater Isopod (isos = equal, pod = foot) which may invade the upper parts of an estuary, but cannot reproduce in salinities greater than 5‰. The 1·5–2 cm ($\frac{3}{5}$–$\frac{4}{5}$ inch) long greyish body is flattened from top to bottom like a wood louse. Water lice are very common in slow moving streams. Unlike freshwater shrimps, they keep well in aquaria without aeration. The eggs are laid in April–May and carried by the female beneath her body. Even after the young have hatched, she still continues to carry them with her. At first the young water lice have no pigmentation and are completely transparent.

Several larvae of freshwater insects (e.g. bugs, beetles and a dragonfly) have been collected from salt marsh pools which flood during HWST. A caddis larva called *Limnephilus affinus* has been

30. Water lice (*Asellus aquaticus*) crawling over fine weeds under water

found several times in brackish water up to 25‰, but it can complete its life history only if the salinity is less than 17‰.

SUMMARY

A few animals which can adapt to a wide salinity range, will live anywhere along the length of the estuary. These include the shore crab, the shrimp, the opossum shrimp *Neomysis*, and the ragworm. In the lower part of the estuary (salinity 30–25‰) mostly marine species are found, including the acorn barnacle, *Balanus*, the edible winkle and the mussel. Both edible winkles and mussels extend into the mid-estuary (25–18‰), where cockles, lugworms, *Corophium*, *Gammarus salinus* and *G. zaddachi* also live. True estuarine or brackish water species occur in the upper region (18–5‰)—*Hydrobia*, the peppery furrow shell, Baltic tellin with *G. zaddachi*, *G. salinus* and *Corophium*. In the head of the estuary where the salinity does not exceed 5‰, the freshwater louse (*Asellus*) occurs.

5. *Animal Visitors and Passers-by*

The last chapter described the animals which either live permanently in estuaries, or else move in for a season and move out to breed. This chapter looks at the European eel (*Anguilla anguilla*) and the salmon, which migrate through, and the birds which visit daily to feed.

FISH

Eels and salmon are two fish which make spectacular migrations between fresh and salt water. The migration pattern differs between the two types of fish. The eel migrates up as a young elver, and migrates down as an adult; whereas the salmon migrates up as an adult to spawn in rivers, and migrates down as an immature fish to feed in the sea.

The distribution of eels and salmon in Britain can be compared in Figures 21 and 22. Each black dot records the presence of the particular species in a 10-kilometre square of the grid used on Ordnance Survey maps. Most of the salmon records are from the western and northern parts of Britain, whereas the eel is more abundant in the south. These maps were produced by the Biological Records Centre of the Nature Conservancy Council, which is collecting and processing the data for many groups of British plants and animals.

(a) *European eel*
To understand the life history of the eel we will start with the adults, which live and feed in fresh water for several years. When in fresh

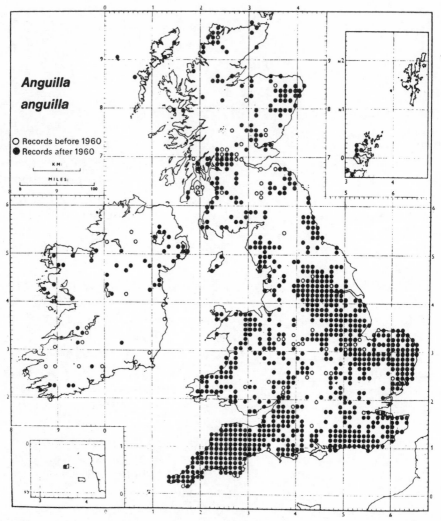

Fig. 21. Map showing distribution of European eel (*Anguilla anguilla*) in the British Isles

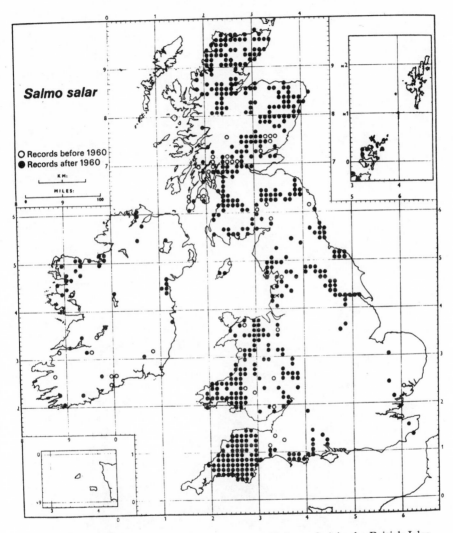

Salmo salar

O Records before 1960
● Records after 1960

KM:

MILES:

Fig. 22. Map showing distribution of salmon (*Salmo salar*) in the British Isles

water they have yellow bellies and are known as 'yellow eels'. In late Summer, when the male eels have reached 40 cm (16 inches) long (7–12 years) and the females up to 60 cm (2 feet) long (9–19 years), they begin to move downstream towards the sea. It is during this downward migration that eels may be seen crawling overland on wet ground. Once in the river the eels tend to move downstream on dark moonless nights after heavy rain.

Eels on their downstream migration begin to change into the 'silver eel' stage. The yellow belly turns silvery and all the sense organs become bigger, the nostrils enlarge, the lateral lines become more obvious and the eyes larger. The reproductive organs also begin to increase in size. The gut begins to degenerate so that the eel can no longer feed.

These silver eels are caught in the Autumn in traps, often built into the mainstream of a river. Once the eels have passed through the estuary and out to sea they are rarely seen again. Very few eels in their breeding dress have been caught at sea, and nobody has seen eels spawning. What is known, however, is that the young larvae

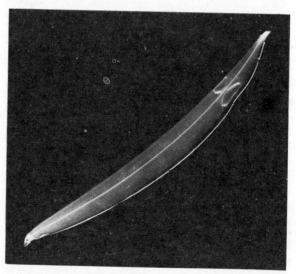

31. Preserved Leptocephalus larva of European eel (*Anguilla anguilla*)

(Leptocephalus larvae), are caught in large numbers in the Sargasso Sea (22–30°N and 48–65°W) in the western part of the Atlantic. So it is assumed that the adult eels take about six months to reach this area, where they spawn and then die.

The flattened leaf-like transparent Leptocephalus larva (Plate 31) was first discovered in 1856. Because it resembled no other known fish, it was given a new generic name, *Leptocephalus*. Forty years later, when two Italian scientists watched some of these larvae change into young eels in an aquarium, it was realised that they were, in fact, the first stage in the life history of the eel.

The actual location of the supposed breeding ground of the European eel was discovered by a Danish marine biologist called Johannes Schmidt. It took him 14 years, from 1906 to 1920, before he concluded that the eels congregated in the Sargasso Sea area. Schmidt did not actually see the eels laying their eggs. Instead he collected and measured Leptocephalus larvae from all over the Atlantic. The largest larvae came from samples taken in the eastern part of the Atlantic and the smallest in a tiny area to the east of America. It was here, he concluded, that the adult eels came to breed. This theory is generally accepted by scientists, but the final con-firmation will come when somebody succeeds in seeing—and possibly photographing—the eels in the act of spawning in the Atlantic.

The Leptocephalus larvae take $2\frac{1}{2}$–3 years to be carried in the Gulf Stream current towards the coast of Europe. During the Winter before they reach our shores they metamorphose into the transparent 'glass eels' or elvers. Elvers have a rounded body like the adult eel. At first they are so transparent that all their inside organs can be seen —the gills, the heart, the gut and the backbone—as shown in Plate 32. Most of the elvers reach rivers which flow into the Atlantic—on the west of Ireland, south-west of Britain and west Spain and Portugal; but some migrate to the more easterly parts of West Europe, and a few even manage to reach the furthest parts of the Baltic.

Elvers begin to reach the Severn Estuary in February, but the main influx takes place in March and April, when they are caught in special elver nets. The fishermen are not out every day—but only when they expect a good elver 'run'. This is usually during the spring

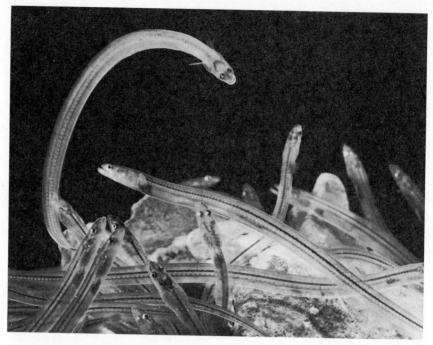

32. Elvers of European eel (*Anguilla anguilla*) writhing up inside of aquarium

tides, about an hour after the tide has ebbed back down towards the sea. Because elvers are much more active at night, most are caught just after the evening high tide. The long-handled, boat-shaped nets are made from a wooden framework with nylon mesh stretched tightly across the base and up the sides.

The elvers swim upstream against the current. They are caught in the net by holding it with the mouth facing out to sea—in the same direction as the current. Because the elvers are so slippery they are poured out of the net into a big bucket rather than picked out by hand. Some are fried and eaten, but most are exported alive to stock inland waters in Europe and Japan.

The wriggling bodies of the elvers can be seen in murky-brown Severn water only when they are swimming actively upstream near the surface. Large numbers may mass together to form a writhing rope when they have to climb up an obstacle, such as a weir, in a shallow depth of water. When they move upstream their bodies gradually darken as the pigment cells begin to develop. The major part of an eel's life is spent in fresh water, where it feeds and grows until it is ready to begin its seaward migration.

(b) *Atlantic Salmon*
The salmon has an equally remarkable life history. Because the salmon breeds in accessible rivers, the act of spawning can be observed quite easily. But to what area of the sea the salmon went to feed was a mystery until quite recently.

Starting once again with the river stage of the life history, it is here that the adult salmon come to spawn. Somehow—possibly by detecting the 'smell' of the river water—they return to the river in which they were born. This has been proved when fish tagged on their downward journey have been recaptured on their return. Plate 33 shows an anaesthetised salmon smolt immediately after tagging.

Because the salmon moves *up* rivers to spawn, it is known as an *anadromous* fish, whereas the eel, which moves *down* rivers to spawn,

33. Tagged salmon (*Salmo salar*) smolt

is a *catadromous* fish. Salmon will live only in clean, well-aerated rivers with a good current.

Salmon spawn in the winter in November and December. The female or hen fish digs out a hollow—known as a redd—in a gravelly bottom. She does this by flexing her body backwards and forwards so that the silt and small stones are swept away in the current. When the work has been done and the redd is 15–30 cm (6–12 inches) deep, the male or cock fish joins the hen. Large cock fish have conspicuous hooked jaws, known as a kype. As the hen lays her orange eggs the cock sheds his white milt, so the eggs become fertilised before they fall in amongst the gravel.

Once they have spawned, the fish—which are known as *kelts*— look thin and some may become infected with 'salmon disease'. Many

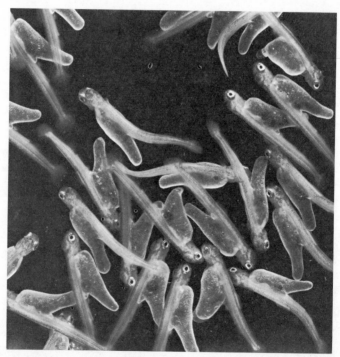

34. Salmon (*Salmo salar*) alevins, four days after hatching showing their large yolk sacs

kelts die as they are carried down river, but some do return to spawn for a second time after feeding in the sea.

In March or early April, in water at 7°C, *alevins*, 16 mm ($\frac{3}{5}$ inch) long, hatch from the eggs about 80–90 days after they are laid. The yellow yolk sac on the underside of the body (Plate 34) is the sole food source for the first four weeks. When the yolk sac has been completely absorbed, and the young fish starts to feed on live food, it is known as a *fry* or *fingerling*. These fry feed and grow for about a year, when they become known as *parr*, which are instantly recognisable by a series of dark blotches along each side of the body. The quicker the parr grow, the sooner they turn into silvery *smolts*. In the Hampshire Avon, this is often after only a year of feeding, whereas in Scottish rivers over half the smolts are 3-year-olds. Whatever age they are, the smolts tend to leave the river in May and June. They move out to sea in large shoals, feeding all the time.

Once in the sea, the smolts feed and grow for 1–4 years, before returning to spawn. Many salmon from British rivers travel across to West Greenland to feed. A salmon which returns after only one year in the sea is known as a *grilse*. The sea fish are silvery blue-green in colour; whereas the river fish are greenish with red or orange mottling. Salmon can enter our rivers during almost any month of the year, but there are definite peak periods. The Cheshire Dee has a big run in March and April, when the salmon are referred to as 'spring fish'. When the peak run happens during the summer, the fish are known as 'summer fish'.

(c) *Salt-water balance control by eel and salmon*

Both eels and salmon have to overcome the problem of moving from fresh water through estuarine to sea water. To be able to do this so successfully clearly means they have some way of controlling their internal salt and water balance—throughout a wide salinity range.

When fish go through an estuary they change over from one type of osmo-regulation to another. The concentration of blood salts of bony fish is equal to 10–14‰ sea water, which is clearly more concentrated than fresh water. When fish are in fresh water, they will have a tendency to take up water from the less concentrated river water. The fish would then tend to swell up; so to counteract this excess of water, they excrete large amounts of dilute urine.

When fish are in the sea, the concentration of their blood salts is less than the surrounding water. Thus fish will tend to lose water to the more concentrated sea water, and become dehydrated. To counteract this, the fish drink a lot of sea water and they also excrete salts through their gills.

Migrating fish remain in the estuary for several days, so they can gradually adjust their salt-water balance.

(d) *Sea trout*

Other migratory fish include the sea trout (*Salmo trutta*), the lampern or river lamprey (*Lampetra fluviatilis*) and the sea lamprey (*Petromyzon marinus*), all of which spawn in rivers.

The sea trout, which is a distinct form of brown trout, makes extensive feeding migrations out to sea. When scales of both forms are examined under a microscope, those of the sea trout show much bigger growth rings during the time they are feeding in the sea.

Like the salmon smolt, the sea trout smolt develop silvery sides before moving out to sea, because their freshwater coloration would be of no survival value in the sea. When they re-enter fresh water (which may be later the same year) they are called *whitlings*. They are not referred to as adult sea trout until after the second summer of seaward migration.

(e) *Lampreys*

The lampern is one of three British species of lampreys. It is larger than the brook lamprey (*Lampetra planeri*) and smaller than the sea lamprey. These eel-like fish have no paired fins and have seven separate gill slits along each side of the front of the body. Lampreys have a skeleton made of cartilage instead of bone, and the adults have round sucking jawless mouths.

The 25–30 cm (10–12 inch) long lamperns spend a year in the sea feeding parasitically on live fish—including salmon—as well as scavenging on dead fish. The structure of the mouth of a mature lampern is shown in Plate 35. In the centre are the jaws, surrounded

35. Circular sucking mouth of adult river lamprey (*Lampetra fluviatilis*) photographed through glass

by a series of teeth plates.

In the Autumn and Spring, lamperns migrate up rivers, where they spawn in April. Once the lampern has moved back into fresh water it can no longer osmo-regulate in sea water. When the fish have reached the spawning area, a slight hollow is excavated by both the male and female removing pebbles from the bottom. The female then anchors herself by her sucking mouth to a stone upstream, so that the male can attach himself to the female's head and wind his body round hers to fertilise the eggs as they are laid. The adults die after they have spawned.

The sea lamprey spawns later in the year, in May and June.

BIRDS

Estuaries are places where the largest concentrations of birds such as waders, ducks and geese gather to feed, especially during the winter months. So for this reason, estuaries are frequented by bird watchers more than any other kind of naturalist. Some of the best places for bird watching on or near estuaries are listed in Section (c) of Chapter 8.

The birds are attracted to estuaries by the large concentrations of invertebrate animals living in the mud banks. On the open flats there is no cover for approaching predators, so the waders can feed safely in huge flocks during the Winter. During the Summer there are still plenty of resident species feeding on the estuarine invertebrates. Birds which come to feed in estuaries can be divided into four distinct groups.

There are the waders which are spectacular from their sheer numbers rather than individual size. The ducks, geese and swans form a distinct second group, while the fish-eating herons, cormorants and the kingfisher comprise the third group. Lastly, there are the gulls, which are both predators and scavengers, and the terns, which are chiefly fish-eaters.

(a) *Waders*

Examples of six different waders have been drawn in Figure 23. Many more are illustrated in the R.S.P.B. Chart No. 7, *Shore birds and waders*. For detailed descriptions of all the birds mentioned in this chapter, you should refer to a bird identification book, such as the one by Heinzel *et al* listed in Section (a) of Chapter 8.

Waders begin to feed as the tide recedes. Shorter-legged waders, such as knot (*Calidris canutus*) and dunlin (*Calidris alpina*), feed on the mud as it becomes exposed; whereas birds like redshank (*Tringa totanus*), curlew (*Numenius arquata*) and avocet (*Recurvirostra avosetta*) use their long legs to wade out to feed in shallow water. In the Autumn waders feed only during the day; but with the onset of short Winter days, they have to feed during the night as well.

The knot (Figure 23f) is one of several species of waders belonging to the genus *Calidris*. It is also one of a much larger group known as sandpipers. Knots reach Britain in late Summer and Autumn from their breeding grounds north of the Arctic Circle. These short greyish (in Winter) waders are midway between the size of redshank and dunlin.

Fig. 23. Some common estuarine birds

(a) Avocet (*Recurvirostra avosetta*)
(b) Shelduck (*Tadorna tadorna*)
(c) Curlew (*Numenius arquata*)
(d) Oystercatcher (*Haematopus ostralegus*)
(e) Dunlin (*Calidris alpina*)
(f) Knot (*Calidris canutus*)

Huge flocks of knots can be seen feeding together on the mud banks
of estuaries in Winter, especially in the Dee Estuary (Cheshire),
Morecambe Bay, Foulness and the Wash. The proposed land reclamation of these areas would seriously threaten a large proportion
of the knots overwintering in Britain. Knots remain closely packed
together even as they fly—when one second the flock is dark and the
next pale, as they wheel round to show their undersides. When in
flight the pale rump and tail show clearly.

It is the bill length which determines the depth down to which
waders can penetrate the mud to feed. Figure 24 compares the bill
length of six waders relative to the burrows of some of the mud-
living invertebrates. Knots, which have a bill length of 30–38 mm
($1\frac{1}{5}$–$1\frac{1}{2}$ inches), feed on crabs, worms and small molluscs.

The dunlin (Figure 23e)—also a sandpiper—is the smallest common wader. In Winter dunlin are grey-brown above, with a dark

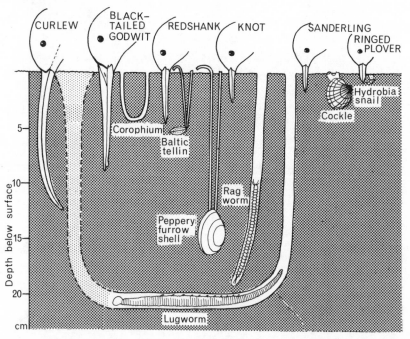

Fig. 24. Diagram to show how the length of waders' bills limits their available food

rump edged in white. The breast is streaked with grey and the underside is white. In Summer they are easy to spot, when they develop a rust back and a black belly. Some dunlin remain in Britain to breed—on moors and marshes—but large flocks fly off to breed in Iceland. Dunlin have a bill length of 25–34 mm ($1-1\frac{2}{5}$ inches) and they feed on small crustaceans and worms.

The black and white oystercatcher (*Haematopus ostralegus*) (Figure 23d), with its long red bill and pink legs, cannot be mistaken for any other bird. Widespread all round the British coast, oystercatchers are especially abundant in the west.

The name oystercatcher is misleading, for it does not feed on oysters which live below LWST. Oystercatchers feed between the tide marks on cockles and mussels and are one of the few waders which do not take their food whole. When mussels are covered by water, their shells are open; therefore the oystercatcher can insert its beak to sever the shell muscle so that the shells open out. When the mussel is exposed, the shells are closed, so the oystercatcher has to use a different technique. It smashes the shell with its beak until it succeeds in breaking the bottom end of the lower valve. Very often pairs of mussel shells with a piece of shell broken from one valve, can be found on the shore.

An oystercatcher eats approximately its own weight each day in mussel or cockle flesh. In Morecambe Bay the rate of feeding varied from 14–51 cockles per hour, with a total of 214–315 cockles being eaten each day by one bird. During the 1954/5 Winter, the 30,000 oystercatchers counted in one part of Morecambe Bay consumed about 22 per cent of the cockles in that area.

About 20,000 pairs of oystercatchers breed in Britain. The nest is merely a scrape in the ground, in which 2–3 eggs are laid amongst shells or pebbles. Oystercatchers will also nest inland on moorland areas, on fields and even on shingle beds beside rivers.

The distinctive 'coorli' call of the curlew (Figure 23c), haunts estuaries and salt marsh areas from mid-Summer to early Spring, when the birds move inland to breed on moors, sand-dunes and heathland areas. This long-legged, long-billed bird is Britain's largest wader. It has a greyish-brown body with a white rump. The

100–152 mm (4–6 inch) long downwardly-curving bill enables it to feed on deep-burrowing lugworms, ragworms and bivalves.

Avocets (Figure 23a) are black-and-white waders with bluish legs and a long black upturned bill. Two hundred years ago these birds used to breed in several places along the east coast. But by draining marshland areas, by collecting eggs to make puddings and by killing the birds themselves for feathers to make into fishing flies, man finally wiped out the last breeding colony by 1825. For more than 100 years, no avocets nested in Britain. Then, after the Second World War, a few pairs began to nest on Minsmere and Havergate Island in the Ore Estuary in Suffolk. Now both these areas are R.S.P.B. reserves and more than 100 pairs of avocets come to nest each Summer on Havergate where a permit is required to visit. The R.S.P.B. has in fact adopted the avocet for its symbol.

Avocets come regularly each year as Winter visitors to the Tamar Estuary, Devon. They use their 75–92 mm (3–3½ inch) long up-turned bill—by sweeping it backwards and forwards through shallow water—to feed on shrimps.

Unlike oystercatchers, which often feed in flocks, the redshank is a more solitary feeder, and has a very varied diet. The redshank's main food is the amphipod, *Corophium volutator*; but it also feeds on ragworms, Baltic tellins, and *Hydrobia* snails.

Other waders which come to feed in estuaries include: the ringed plover (*Charadrius hiaticula*), throughout the year; the grey plover (*Pluvialis squatarola*), sanderling (*Calidris alba*), and turnstone (*Arenaria interpres*), all as Winter visitors; and the whimbrel (*Numenius phaeopus*) and greenshank (*Tringa nebularia*), as migrants passing through in Spring and Autumn.

(b) *Ducks, geese and swans*
Britain's largest duck—the shelduck (*Tadorna tadorna*) (Figure 23b) —frequents estuaries throughout the greater part of the year. Most of them leave our shores in July to moult on Heligoland in the German Bight, but a few assemble in Bridgwater Bay to moult. Both the drake (male) and the duck (female) have a very striking plumage, with portions of chestnut, white and black.

Shelduck move up and down the shoreline with the tide. Once the tide has turned, they move down to feed, especially on *Hydrobia* snails, while at high tide they rest either on the shore or on the sea. The shelduck, like the mallard (*Anas platyrhynchos*), loses all its flight feathers when it moults each year. At this stage it cannot fly until the new feathers have grown; so it simply floats in up the shore with the rising tide.

By contrast, the teal (*Anas crecca*) is Britain's smallest native duck. It moves into estuaries and mud flats in winter to feed on a variety of food, including glasswort.

Other duck found in estuaries are the eider (*Somateria mollissima*) and scaup (*Aythya marila*). The eider drake is black and white, while the duck is mottled brown in colour. The light, fluffy down feathers, which the duck plucks from her breast to line the nest, are the original stuffing of eiderdowns. Eiders feed on molluscs and crabs. The largest colonies of eider are on the Farne Islands, at the mouth of the Tay and in the Ythan Estuary.

During the Winter, scaup form very large flocks on Scottish firths,

36. Barnacle goose (*Branta leucopsis*)

especially the Firth of Forth. They dive down through the water to feed on mussels. In May these duck move northwards to their breeding grounds in the Arctic.

Geese, which are generally larger than ducks, have long necks. They are typically gregarious birds which move around in flocks. The barnacle goose (*Branta leucopsis*) (Plate 36) is a small grey goose, intermediate in size between the brent and Canada goose (*Branta canadensis*), with a black neck and white face. Up to 3,000 overwinter in Scotland, mainly in the Western Isles and some at Caerlaverock National Nature Reserve on the Solway Firth.

Barnacle geese feed on grassy areas behind sand-dunes. Their name is derived from the mythical medieval belief that the birds came forth from goose barnacles—relatives of the acorn barnacles described on page 56.

Ten to twenty thousand of the dark-bellied race of brent geese come from Siberia to overwinter in Britain. While a few brent geese go to the River Medway, Kent, the Norfolk coast and Langstone Harbour, Hampshire, most of them—over one third of the total world population—go to Foulness. Twelve thousand of the light-bellied race come from Greenland to overwinter in Ireland.

Brent geese feed almost exclusively on eel-grass, and so they were directly hit by the eel-grass disease of the 1930s. The geese then turned to feed on the green alga, *Enteromorpha*, but as this does not grow so extensively as the eel-grass, the numbers of brent geese dropped markedly. It was not until the 1954 Protection of Birds Act was passed, making it illegal to shoot brent geese in Britain, that the numbers began to recover. Beds of eel-grass are now becoming established in many estuaries.

More than 5,000 pink-footed geese (*Anser brachyrhynchus*) over-winter—mainly in the Firth of Forth in Scotland. Some also reach the Wash and the Humber. Pink-footed geese are the only grey geese with both pink legs and a pink bill. Some greylag geese (*Anser anser*) breed naturally in the Outer Hebrides and the extreme north of Scotland. Many more fly south to Scotland from their Icelandic breeding grounds.

Mute swans (*Cygnus olor*) are so widely distributed throughout

37. Mute swan (*Cygnus olor*) tracks at edge of estuary

38. Herring gull (*Larus argentatus*)

D

Britain that they cannot be regarded as typically estuarine birds. None the less, they often frequent estuaries, where they leave their tell-tale footprints in the mud (Plate 37).

All the mute swans on the River Thames belong to the Dyers' Company, the Vintners' Company or to the Queen. In July or August, the swan-upping ceremony—continued since the reign of Elizabeth I —takes place. All the cygnets which are owned by either of the two companies are marked on the bill; all those that are left unmarked belong to the Queen.

(c) *Gulls*

The wailing 'keeow' cry of the herring gull (*Larus argentatus*) (Plate 38) is a sound which everyone associates with the seashore. The gulls scavenge on garbage, and prey on crabs and shellfish, as well as the eggs and chicks of other birds. In estuaries, the gulls can be seen quartering the shore for floating rubbish. They also attack crabs and mussels by repeatedly dropping them from a height until they eventually hit a rock and break open.

Black-headed gulls (*Larus ridibundus*), which incidentally lose their black heads in Winter, will also visit estuaries. Plate 39 shows a flock taking off from saltings in Sussex at low tide.

39. Black-headed gulls (*Larus ridibundus*) taking off from Sussex salt marsh in July

6. *Man and Estuaries*

sᴚᴚᴚᴚᴚᴚᴚᴚᴚᴚᴚᴚᴚᴚᴚᴚᴚᴚᴚ

Man both uses and abuses estuaries. Much of man's exploitation is seriously detrimental to the environment, but some of his uses are less damaging. His influence will be considered under the following five headings: recreation, industry, fisheries, pollution and con-servation.

(a) *Recreation*

Estuaries are exploited for recreation in many ways, such as fishing, sailing, water ski-ing and power boat racing. These recreational activities are not always compatible; for instance, the fishing is spoilt if water ski-ing and power boat racing take place simultaneously on the same stretch of water. Even apparently harmless pursuits can have damaging consequences: the rapid increase in the popularity of sailing is resulting in the building of marinas and more slipways.

Perhaps the ancient sport of angling is the least harmful to the environment. Grey mullet and flounders are the most commonly caught regular inhabitants. Shoals of grey mullet move up estuaries, with each fish making a characteristic V-shaped ripple on the water surface with its dorsal fin. These fish, or any others near the surface, can be seen more clearly through Polaroid sunglasses which, like a polarising filter placed over the camera lens, help to cut down the reflections and glare on the water surface.

Mullet feed naturally on fine green seaweeds and microscopic plants. They can be caught with extraordinary baits such as banana, macaroni, cheese and even boiled cabbage stalks! In contrast, flounders are inquisitive fish which can be attracted to any disturbance on the bottom. A spoon (a rounded spinning disc) with ragworm as bait, or a lead weight on the bottom of a line dragged along the bottom, will lure them.

The decline in the popularity of wildfowling and the corresponding increase in nature photography and bird watching shows our growing awareness of the need to conserve our wild life.

(b) *Industry*

Historically, estuaries have been important as protected harbours and anchorages. The ready availability of raw materials brought in by sea, and the existence of radiating communication systems both overland and by sea, encourage the development of industry on estuaries. Land prices are now so high in Britain that it is often cheaper to reclaim land in an estuary than to buy an inland site for a factory. This ever-increasing demand for raw materials and energy to feed British industry, means that the size of vessels entering estuaries is increasing, so that deeper channels have to be dredged.

40. Recreation and industrialisation together in an estuary. A boy fishing and the Milford Haven oil refinery behind

When oil refineries are built on estuaries, the expense of overland pipe lines is avoided. The crude oil brought in by tankers is off-loaded at deep-water quays as at Milford Haven (Plate 40) or further offshore into pipe lines, as at Fawley in Southampton Water. For similar reasons oil-fired power stations are being built on estuaries. At Inverkip on the Firth of Clyde, 80,000-ton tankers will supply the £94 million power station.

One of the major requirements of power stations is cooling water to condense the steam which is used to drive the turbines. A 2,000-megawatt power station, operated by burning coal or oil, requires 50 million gallons of cooling water per hour, when running at full output. As the cooling water cools down the steam, it becomes warmed up by about 10°C, and so is discharged back into the estuary as warm water. Most of the inland power stations have large unsightly cooling towers built to condense their steam.

The first generation of nuclear power stations required about 50 per cent more cooling water than coal or oil-fired stations. This is why the majority were sited on estuaries where there is a constant supply of cooling water. Nuclear power stations on estuaries include Hinkley Point, Oldbury-on-Severn (Plate 41) and Berkeley on the

41. Oldbury-on-Severn nuclear power station

Severn and Hunterston A on the Clyde. The second generation of nuclear power stations, such as Hunterston B, however, utilise gas-cooled reactors and require about the same quantity of cooling water, per unit of electricity generated, as coal and oil-fired stations.

The conventional coal-fired power station at Kincardine on the Firth of Forth was built on reclaimed land. It produces 1,500 tonnes of furnace and fly ash a day—much of which is being used for further land reclamation. One of the largest schemes for land reclamation now being studied is the plan to build a third London airport and port on Maplin Sands, in the Thames Estuary. The Government has already spent £$\frac{3}{4}$ million on studying what the effects will be on tide and currents in the estuary, if a 25-kilometre (15 mile) sea wall is built and 300–400 million cubic yards of sand are dredged from Barrow Bank to raise the level. Since the mean sea level is rising at Southend by 0·4 m (15$\frac{3}{4}$ inches) per century and 0·7 m (27$\frac{1}{2}$ inches) per century at Tower Bridge, it is important to assess the effects of such schemes on any freak high tides caused by storm surges in the North Sea. A barrage across the Thames at London is being planned to prevent the ever-increasing likelihood of serious flooding as a result of a storm surge. Normally the barrage would be open to allow the tides to ebb and flow, and it would be closed only when an abnormally high tide is predicted.

Other barrage schemes are being explored in theory for Morecambe Bay, the Dee Estuary (Cheshire) and the Wash. Industrial demands for water are outstripping Britain's supplies. One way of increasing the water supply is to build more reservoirs, but this means drowning river valleys and farming land. A barrage built across Morecambe Bay would keep out sea water and retain fresh river water. The Morecambe Bay scheme alone would store 7,500 gallons and allow 500 million gallons of fresh water to be drawn per day. The barrage could provide a roadway to the depressed area around Barrow, but fisheries and bird-feeding grounds would be destroyed and Heysham harbour would silt up. A better alternative for preserving the wildlife would be a storage reservoir along the shore of the estuary.

(c) *Fisheries*

Many commercial shell fisheries are based on estuaries. With the exception of salmon, sea trout and eels, fish are not caught on a commercial scale in estuaries. The most important commercial shell-fish are cockles, mussels and oysters. Shrimps are also caught in estuaries, as described on page 54.

Edible cockles are collected by raking from the Burry Inlet in Carmarthen Bay, the Dee (Cheshire) Estuary, Morecambe Bay and at Boston on the Wash. Mussels are also collected from Morecambe Bay and Boston, as well as from the Menai Straits and the Conway Estuary.

Several estuaries along the Essex coast, including the Blackwater, Crouch and Roach, used to support a good oyster population. But owing to severe winters, predation by sting winkles (*Ocenebra erinacea*) and competition with the slipper limpet (*Crepidula fornicata*) the oyster beds have declined rather than flourished. The settling larvae of bivalve shellfish are known as 'spat'. Most of the oysters in this country—especially in the Helford Estuary, Cornwall, are grown from spat imported from France.

Both shellfish and fish will grow faster in warm water. Experiments are now being carried out to see which British and foreign species grow best in warm water effluents emerging from estuarine power stations. At the Marine Farm at Hinkley Point power station, both native and Pacific oysters (*Crassostrea gigas*) are reared in trays in special outdoor ponds (Plate 42), as well as large-sized tiger prawns (*Panaeus japonicus*) imported from Japan. Oysters filter-feed on plant plankton, so their tanks are periodically 'seeded' with algal cultures. The prawns are fed with a paste made from mincing the fish caught on the screens that have been put across the cooling water intake to the power station.

Salmon are caught in estuaries in a variety of ways. The most widely used method is by Seine netting them on the ebbing tide. This can be seen at Mudeford on the Avon Estuary near Christchurch between 1st February and 31st July. Two fishermen work the net. One stands on the bank holding a rope attached to one end of the net.

42. Lifting out a tray of Pacific oysters (*Crassostrea gigas*) from warm water pond at the Marine Farm, Hinkley Point. The new B station is in the background

43. Paying out a Seine net at Mudeford on Avon Estuary, Hampshire

The other rows out from the shore paying out the long net into the water (Plate 43). One edge of the net is weighted, while the other is buoyed up with floats, so that the net forms a curtain from the top to the bottom of the water. When all the net is paid out, the oarsman rows back to the shore with the rope attached to the other end of the net. Once he is ashore, both fishermen pull on the ends of the net so that it forms a loop (Plate 44) and is slowly pulled ashore. Net after net may be pulled in without a single fish being caught, and then suddenly several fish are hauled out at once (Plate 45).

44. Pulling in Seine net

45. Landed salmon in Seine net

46. A fisherman walking out at low tide to inspect salmon putcheon weir beneath Severn Bridge

In the Severn Estuary, salmon are caught in putcheons. These wicker-work, funnel-shaped baskets are attached in rows to a weir of stakes running at right angles to the estuary (Plate 46). The mouth of each putcheon faces upstream and the whole weir is covered at high water. Any fish which becomes caught in the putcheons are collected at low water. Putcheons, or 'putts' as they are known locally, can be seen at low water just beneath the Severn Bridge and at Awre. Another method which a few Severn fishermen still use for catching salmon is by means of a curious lave-net. The large net is attached to a Y-shaped frame, which is held in the hand.

(d) *Pollution*
The concentration of industry and centres of population on estuaries, inevitably results in the increase in their pollution. If sewage and processed sludge is dumped into water, bacteria will feed on it and utilise much of the oxygen, so that fish and other animals then die

from lack of oxygen. The number of dangerous bacteria also is increased. Sewage sludge, together with industrial waste, contains increased concentrations of heavy metal ions such as lead, mercury, zinc, cadmium and copper. Certain organisms can concentrate these ions to the extent that they may become poisonous to anyone eating them. The most notorious example of this was at Minimata in Japan, where people died through eating shellfish contaminated with mercury.

Oil is clearly a dangerous pollutant. Over 1,000 eider ducks died from oil pollution in the Tay Estuary in 1968, and more recently, in June 1973, the 100,000-ton *Conoco Britannia* ran aground spilling oil into the Humber Estuary. Minor spills are common around oil

47. Aerial view of Adur Estuary, Shoreham-by-Sea, Sussex. Note the power station with the tall chimneys

refineries and can be controlled with the new non-toxic detergents developed as a result of research done after the *Torrey Canyon* disaster. A major oil spill, however, would still cause devastating damage to amenities, to wildlife and to fisheries. Fish tainted with oil are unsaleable for months after being contaminated.

Even warm water discharged from power stations into an estuary can be considered to be a form of pollution. The higher temperature speeds up the heart beat, the respiration rate and the metabolism in general of an organism, and therefore changes the whole ecology of the area around the discharge outlets. The Central Electricity Generating Board's Marine Biological Laboratory, which was opened at the oil-powered Fawley station in Southampton Water in 1969, is concerned with the effects of warm water effluents. We have already seen on page 103 how warm water effluents can be utilised to advantage for fish farming.

The apparently harmless fly ash sometimes discharged from power stations as a slurry into the estuary can cover the rich mud banks with an inert sterile blanket, stifling the inhabitants.

(e) *Conservation*

Awareness of the dangers of pollution is now resulting in counter measures. In the Thames these have been particularly effective. The Thames had become, slowly but steadily, an open sewer. Untreated sewage was pumped into the water, and by the 1850s the stench was so bad that sheets soaked in disinfectant had to be hung outside the Houses of Parliament. Cholera epidemics broke out in 1853, 1866 and 1870.

Sewage works were built, but were inadequate to cope with the increase in population and industrial effluents. Bacteria feeding on the waste first used up the oxygen, then produced hydrogen sulphide which blackens water and mud, smells of bad eggs and kills nearly all life. In 1957 a survey carried out between Richmond and Gravesend found that no fish except eels were present.

In 1962 the Port of London Authority took over responsibility for controlling pollution in the Thames. The controls worked. As the oxygen levels increased, the fish and birds began to return. Despite the 16 larger sewage works and 23 power stations along the banks of the Thames, 63 species of fish have now been recorded from the tidal Thames; the largest being a 48-lb cod (*Gadus morhua*), an 8-lb bass (*Dicentrarchus* [= *Morone*] *labrax*) and a $3\frac{3}{4}$-lb sea-trout.

Birds which previously by-passed the Thames are also returning. A survey carried out in the Winter of 1971 by the London Natural History Society reported several species of duck and large numbers of waders, including 5,600 dunlin, 1,500 lapwing (*Vanellus vanellus*) and 1,000 redshank.

One of the problems is to find out what life is present to conserve. This may involve large numbers of people over many years: for example, the Birds of Estuaries Survey (see page 112), and the exten sion of the original terrestrial mapping scheme (page 79) to include coastal species. Once such data has been collected, any particularly interesting or rich areas can then be set aside as Reserves, to prevent them from being developed. The National Nature Reserves located on estuaries are listed under Section (c) of Chapter 8. Other types of reserves, such as the Wildfowl Trust at Slimbridge, may be initiated by the enthusiasm of a single individual.

It is essential that potential pollution threats should be identified *before* they damage the estuarine environment. Rivers and estuaries are constantly monitored and controlled by the River Authorities. Also various research laboratories, such as the G.E.C.B. Marine Laboratory at Fawley, are continually obtaining more information about the limits which natural inhabitants can tolerate without being harmed or killed.

7. *Studying an Estuary*

Having read about many of the plants and animals which live in estuaries, and how man has influenced the growth and development of estuaries and, in some cases, brought about their pollution, you may like to undertake investigations about your own estuary. A few suggestions are given below. Firstly, a word of warning. Plate 48 shows you how treacherous the mud flats are. NEVER walk out over the flats on your own, and always walk where seaweeds or other plants are growing.

48. Beware—mud flats are dangerous!

(1) *Questions to answer*

Where is your nearest estuary, and what is it called?

Has it always had this name?

By what means does man cross from one side to the other?

What is the distance across the mouth?

How deep is the channel?

What size of ships pass up it, and during what state of the tide?

Is there a power station on the estuary?

Are there any signs of pollution?

If so, from where did they originate?

Is the estuary used for any recreational purposes?

Are any shellfish or fish collected from the estuary for sale?

If so, how are they collected, and at what time of year?

Where are the shellfish or fish eaten—locally or in other parts of
   Britain or Europe?

What kinds of birds come to the estuary?

Do the birds stay there throughout the year, or do they change during
the seasons?

What plants grow in your estuary?

Please send any interesting discoveries you make about your estuary
to:

Heather Angel, c/o Faber and Faber Ltd., 3 Queen Square, London
WC1N 3AU.

(2) *Tidal measurements*

Find a post or a pier support on which levels have been marked.
Check whether these marks are in feet or in metres. Time how long
the water takes to rise (or fall) from one mark to another. Note the
level every 15 minutes for a 2-hourly period on either side of low
water or high water. Does the water rise (or fall) at a constant rate?

   Look up the exact time of low water (or high water) in tide tables.
Measure the vertical rise (or fall) between high and low water, by
noting the water level at the time of high water and the level at the
time of low water. The difference between these two heights will give
you the tidal range for that particular day. Try to do this during the

spring tide period, and then repeat it during the neap tide period. Compare the tidal range for both times and see how well your ranges match the range given in tide tables.

(3) *Bird Survey*

Make a list of all the birds which come to your estuary throughout the year. These can be ticked off on the check-list printed in the R.S.P.B. Bird Watcher's Field Note Book (15 pence). Keep a separate note of which months of the year you see each species. Watch the birds with binoculars to see how they fly.

49. Bird watchers

Also see how they feed and what they feed on.
How do they use their bills and feet?
There is a national Birds of Estuaries Survey being undertaken jointly by the B.T.O. and the R.S.P.B. (addresses given on page 117). The aim is to record the numbers of birds, especially waders, which visit each estuary.

(4) *Plant Survey*

Make a large-scale map of part of one shore of your estuary. A salt marsh area is a good place, and it will be easier to identify the plants in June or July when most of them are flowering. Make a smaller scale map on graph paper to take with you in to the field. On this second map plot the distribution of the common plants— especially those mentioned in Chapter 3. Use a different symbol for each species, as shown in Figure 10.

Even if you cannot identify every plant, give each one a symbol and make a note of the size of the plant, the colour of the flowers (if any), and at what level on the shore it was growing. Also draw a rough sketch of the plant in your field note book.

Where do the brown seaweeds end and the first flowering plants begin to grow? Can you see some sort of zonation of the plants? If so, does this show up on your map?

When you have completed your survey, transfer the symbols, perhaps by using different coloured pencils, to your larger scale map. Draw on this the high water and low water levels either from your own observations, or else from the $2\frac{1}{2}$-inch Ordnance Survey map. These maps give the HWMOT level (High Water Mark of Ordinary Tides) and the LWMOT (Low Water Mark of Ordinary Tides).

What final conclusions can you make about your own Survey? Another way of making a survey, showing how the distribution of species change along a line, is to do a profile, like the one in Figure 10. This is compiled by noting the plants growing in a straight line from the lowest part of the shore which you can reach safely on foot, up the shore at right angles to the estuary.

The rise and fall of the land level should be measured by using three surveying poles, marked off in centimetres. One pole is held horizontally, along the transect line, while the other two are held vertically at either end of the first. The difference in height of the land at each end of the horizontal pole can then be measured and recorded, to scale, on a large sheet of graph paper.

(5) Food chains

The food of the different animals described in this book has already been mentioned. But what is even more interesting is to work out the succession of feeding levels which form a *food chain.*

A simple food chain can be made by starting first of all with a

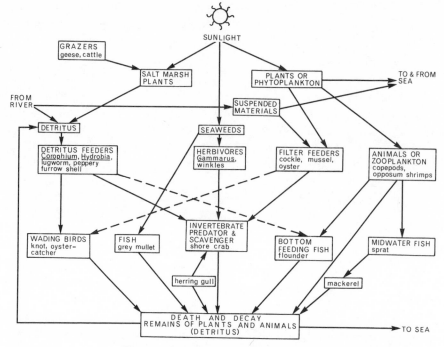

Fig. 25. Generalised estuarine food web

plant, listing an animal which feeds on it (a herbivore) and finally noting an animal which feeds on the herbivore. Figure 25 is more than a simple straight line food chain. It is a *food web*, which illustrates lots of interactions between estuarine plants and animals. Notice how all the plants and animals finally die and decay to form *detritus*, which is utilised by the detritus feeders.

Figure 25 can be used as a summary to Chapters 3, 4 and 5. By using this as a guide, try to compile your own food chain or web from *your own observations*.

(6) *Collecting Shells*

Although estuaries do not have the variety of shells that can be found on the open coast, several different kinds of molluscs live in estuaries. These can be identified from Nora McMillan's book, *British Shells*.

If your record is to be of any scientific value, you should list the following information on a piece of card, which should be stored in a box with the shell.

- (a) *Date* you found the shell. Give the day, month and year
- (b) *Locality* where it was found, with the Ordnance Survey grid reference
- (c) *Type of shore* (rock, sand or mud)
- (d) *Shore level* (see page 30)
- (e) *Abundance.* Was this the only one of its kind, or were there others?

You may also like to draw or photograph the shells. See how many of the shells you find are bivalve and how many are univalve shells. A guide to *Collecting British Marine Molluscs* is published by the Conchological Society, whose address is given under Section 10 below. This guide explains how to submit records for the Conchological Society's Marine Census.

(7) *Footprints*
Lots of visitors to estuaries leave their impressions in the mud, for instance, the swan tracks shown in Plate 37. Look for footprints of other birds and draw or photograph them. Alternatively, make a cast of the footprints from plaster of Paris which can be bought from a chemist. Some sort of frame—preferably metal—will be needed to contain the plaster of Paris when it is poured on to the tracks. After the plaster has been poured in, it should be left for at least 15–20 minutes to set hard. This method gives you a *negative* impression of the print, which can be shown more clearly by painting the footprint impressions with a coloured paint.

(8) *Mussel feeding experiment*
Collect some live mussels and put them into a bowl or an aquarium of sea or estuarine water. If the estuary water is murky, filter it through a pad of cotton wool wedged into a filter funnel. Dissolve a pinch of dried or natural yeast in a cup of warm water with a teaspoon of sugar, and add a drop of a tincture of iodine to colour the starch produced by the yeast, a blue-black colour. Pipette a few drops of

50. Edible mussels (*Mytilus edulis*) with open valves
feeding under water

this solution near the open valves of a mussel. Watch the coloured
stream being drawn in through the frilly inhalent siphon (see Plate
50) and notice that no coloured liquid is ejected from the mussel.
Why is this? Notice also how much smaller the plain exhalent siphon
is than the frilly siphon. This smaller opening ensures that the waste
products are ejected out of the mussel with a greater force than the
fresh supply of water is drawn in—so that the two streams do not
become mixed.

(9) *Photography*

In this book there are examples of *landscape* photography (views), *aerial* photography (from an aircraft), *close-up* photography (with a close-up lens or an extension tube), and *aquarium* photography. The techniques for each type of photography are quite different, and if you want to read more about these you should refer to my detailed book on photography, listed on page 120.

General habitat photographs, such as Plates 2, 3, 4 and 40, are the easiest kinds of photographs to take—with any sort of camera. These are useful for showing how the appearance of an estuary can change during different seasons as well as different states of the tide.

(10) *Societies to join*

If you are interested in natural history in general, you will benefit by joining your local Natural History Society or your County Naturalists' Trust. Then, if you begin to develop an interest in one aspect of natural history, you may decide to join a specialist society. Some of those which are most relevant to this book are listed below.

The British Ichthyological Society (Fishes)
Hon. Secretary: D. Marlborough, Esq.,
                   42 Stanborough Green,
                   Welwyn Garden City,
                   Hertfordshire.

The British Trust for Ornithology
Beech Grove, Tring, Hertfordshire.

The Conchological Society of Great Britain and Ireland (Shells and Molluscs)

Hon. Secretary: Mrs. E. B. Rands,
                   51 Wychwood Avenue,
                   Luton,
                   Bedfordshire LU2 7HT.

The Royal Society for the Protection of Birds
The Lodge, Sandy, Bedfordshire, SG19 2DL.

Wildfowl Trust
Slimbridge, Gloucestershire, GL2 7BT.

For details of junior membership, apply directly to each society.

8. *Further Reading and Information*

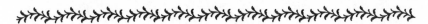

There are no simple guides to estuaries, but this chapter will help those readers who want to learn more about estuaries in general. If some of the books listed in the first two sections are not in your own school library, then perhaps they can be borrowed or referred to at your local library or museum.

(a) *Books for Identification*
This first section lists some of the reference books available for identifying the plants, marine and freshwater life, shells, fishes and birds which can be found in estuaries.

Bagenal, T. B., *The Observer's Book of Sea Fishes*, rev. edn., Warne, London, 1972.

Barrett, J. H. and Yonge, C. M., *Pocket Guide to the Seashore*, Collins, London, 1958.

Beedham, G. E., *Identification of the British Mollusca*, Hulton Educational, Amersham, 1972.

Dickinson, C. I., *British Seaweeds*, Eyre & Spottiswoode, London, 1963.

Ellis, E. A., *Wild Flowers of the Coast*, Jarrold Colour Publications, Norwich, 1973.

Engelhardt, W., *The Young Specialist Looks at Pond Life*, Burke, London, 1964.

Haas, de W. and Knorr, F., *The Young Specialist Looks at Marine Life*, Burke, London, 1966.

Heinzel, H., Fitter, R. and Parslow, J., *The Birds of Britain and Europe*, Collins, London, 1972.

Hepburn, I., *Flowers of the Coast*, Collins, London, 1952.

Maitland, P. S., *Key to the British Freshwater Fishes*, Freshwater Biological Association, Scientific Publication No. 27, 1972.

Martin, W. Keble, *The Concise British Flora in Colour*, Ebury Press, London, 1965.

McMillan, N. F., *British Shells*, Warne, London, 1968.

Mellanby, H., *Animal Life in Fresh Water*, 6th edn., Methuen, London, 1963.

Nichols, D. and Cooke, J. A. L., *The Oxford Book of Invertebrates*, O.U.P., London, 1971.

Tebble, N., *British Bivalve Seashells*, British Museum (Nat. Hist.), London, 1966.

(b) *Books for General Reading*

These include books for readers who want to discover in more detail about some aspects of estuaries which have interested them in this book.

Admiralty Tide Tables, Vol. 1, European Waters, published annually by the Hydrographer to the Navy.

Angel, H., *Nature Photography : its art and techniques*, Fountain Press/ M.A.P., Kings Langley, 1972.

Eltringham, S. K., *Life in Mud and Sand*, English Universities Press, London, 1971.

Ennion, E. A. R. and Tinbergen, N., *Tracks*, O.U.P., London, 1967.

Evans, S. M. and Hardy, J. M., *Seashore and Sand Dunes*, Heinemann Educational Books, London, 1970.

Fisher, J. and Lockley, R. M., *Sea Birds*, Collins, London, 1954.

Flegg, J., *Discovering Bird Watching*, Shire Publications, Aylesbury, 1973.

Gooders, J., *Where to Watch Birds*, André Deutsch, London, 1967.

Green, J., *The Biology of Estuarine Animals*, Sidgwick & Jackson, London, 1968.

Jones, J. W., *The Salmon*, Collins, London, 1959.

McLusky, D. S., *Ecology of Estuaries*, Heinemann Educational Books, London, 1971.

Pilkington, R., *The Ways of the Sea*, Routledge & Kegan Paul, London, 1957.

Port of London Authority, *The Cleaner Thames*, 1966.

Rowbotham, F., *The Severn Bore*, 2nd edn., David & Charles, Newton Abbot, 1970.

Soper, T., *The Shell Book of Beachcombing*, David & Charles, Newton Abbot, 1972.

Tansley, A. G., (revised by M. C. F. Proctor), *Britain's Green Mantle*, 2nd edn., George Allen and Unwin, London, 1968.

Tricker, R. A. R., *Bores, breakers, waves and wakes*, Mills & Boon, London, 1964.

Yonge, C. M., *The Sea Shore*, rev. edn. Collins, London, 1966.

(c) *Interesting Places to Visit*

Some of the places listed below are National Nature Reserves (NNR). The ones for which there are leaflets available from the Nature Conservancy Council (f) are marked with an asterisk. These leaflets describe the plants and animals (especially the birds) which you are likely to see, and also tells you whether you have to apply for a permit to visit the particular Reserve. Nearly all the places listed here are described with directions of how to reach them by road, in John Gooders' book, *Where to Watch Birds*.

ENGLAND

Cheshire
Dee Estuary and Hilbre Island
Mersey Estuary
Weaver Estuary

Cornwall
Camel Estuary
Fal Estuary
Hayle Estuary

Devonshire
Axe Estuary

*Braunton Burrows NNR
Exe Estuary
Kingsbridge Estuary
Plym Estuary
Tamar Estuary
Torridge—Taw Estuary
Yealm Estuary

Dorset
Brownsea Island (owned by the
   National Trust)

Essex
Blackwater Estuary
Bradwell Bird Observatory
Canvey Point, Thames Estuary
Dengie Flats, between Rivers
   Blackwater and Crouch
Tollesbury, on mouth of River
   Blackwater

Gloucestershire
Severn Beach
Wildfowl Trust, Slimbridge

Hampshire and the Isle of Wight
Langstone Harbour and
   Farlington Marshes
Newtown Marsh, Isle of Wight

Kent
Cliffe
Medway Estuary

Lancashire
Alt Estuary
Duddon Estuary
Keer Estuary
Kent Estuary
Leven Estuary
Morecambe Bay

Lincolnshire
The Wash area

Norfolk
Blakeney Point
Breydon Water
*Holkham NNR
*Scolt Head Island NNR

Northumberland
Tweed Estuary
Tynemouth

Somerset
Axe Estuary
*Bridgwater Bay NNR

Suffolk
Alde—Orde Estuary
Blyth Estuary
Deben Estuary
Havergate Island (R.S.P.B.
   Reserve)
Orwell Estuary
Stour Estuary

Sussex
Chichester Harbour
Cuckmere Haven
Pagham Harbour

Yorkshire
Humber Wildfowl Refuge

WALES

*Newborough Warren NNR
  (Anglesey)
Conway Estuary
  (Caernarvonshire)
Shotton Pools (Flintshire)
*Dyfi NNR (Dovey Estuary,
  Cardiganshire)
Taf, Towy and Gwendraeth
  Estuaries (Carmarthenshire)
Teifi Estuary (Cardiganshire)
Taff Estuary, Penarth Flats
  (Glamorganshire)
*Whiteford NNR
  (Glamorganshire)
Mawddach Estuary
  (Merionethshire)
*Morfa Dyffryn NNR
  (Merionethshire)
*Morfa Harlech NNR
  (Merionethshire)
Usk Estuary (Monmouthshire)
Milford Haven (Pembrokeshire)

SCOTLAND

Findhorn Bay (Morayshire)
Spey Mouth (Morayshire)
*Sands of Forvie NNR
  (Aberdeenshire)
Eden Estuary (Fifeshire)
Firth of Tay (Fifeshire)
Aberlady Bay (East Lothian)
Tyne Mouth (East Lothian)
Beauly Firth (Ross & Cromarty)
Cromarty Firth (Ross &
  Cromarty)
Dornoch Firth (Ross &
  Cromarty)
*Invernaver NNR (Sutherland)
Kyle of Tongue and Roan
  Island (Sutherland)
Inner Moray Firth (Ross &
  Cromarty)
*Caerlaverock NNR
  (Dumfriesshire)
Mersehead Sands
  (Kirkcudbrightshire)
Rough Firth
  (Kirkcudbrightshire)
Wigtown Bay
  (Kirkcudbrightshire/
  Wigtownshire)

(d) *Bird Song Recordings*

One way of identifying birds in the field is to learn to recognise their calls. There are now several records available with very good recordings of bird songs. The list below is especially relevant for estuarine birds.

Listen the birds . . . (Series available from the R.S.P.B.)
No. 8. Common sandpiper/Snipe/Woodcock/Golden Plover/Curlew/
Lapwing/Oystercatcher/Redshank/Wader Chorus.
No. 16. Grey plover/Dotterel/Ringed Plover/Whimbrel/Turnstone/
Spotted Redshank/Greenshank/Knot/Sanderling.

Estuary Birds. A Shell Nature Record:
British Bird Series DCL 704

Wildlife of East Anglia, Wildlife Series:
B.B.C. Records RED 83M

(e) *Wallchart*
R.S.P.B. Chart No. 7. *Shorebirds and Waders.* (Distributed by the
R.S.P.B. and Warne, London)

(f) *Useful addresses*
Estuarine and Brackish Water Biological Association
c/o Department of Zoology,
 University of Cambridge,
 Downing Street,
 Cambridge CB2 3EJ.

The headquarters of the *Nature Conservancy Council* are as follows:

 England
 19 Belgrave Square, London, SW1X 8PY
 Scotland
 12 Hope Terrace, Edinburgh, EH9 2AS.
 Wales
 Penrhos Road, Bangor, Caernarvonshire

Society for the Promotion of Nature Reserves (SPNR—co-ordinators
of the County Naturalists' Trusts)
The Manor House, Alford, Lincolnshire.

6/82/N

Index

6/82/N